THE CATHOLIC MILIEU

by Thomas Storck

CHRISTENDOM COLLEGE PRESS
Route 3, Box 87
Front Royal, VA 22630

ISBN Number: 0-931888-25-5
©1987 Christendom Educational Corporation

To my Wife

Wer ein holdes Weib errungen . . .

-Schiller

CONTENTS

INTRODUCTION

In recent years, Catholics have become increasingly conscious of the clash between Catholicism as a *general* culture,
and the culture of the world around them. The work of men
like Belloc, Maritain, Christopher Dawson and others, has
shown that we differ not in religion alone, but in the whole
realm of unspoken and spontaneous things, which color even
our daily routine.

— George Bull, S.J.[1]

My purpose in this work is to set forth and explain what
"Catholicism as a *general* culture" is. I believe that there is such
a thing as Catholic culture, that is, a way of life brought into
being and fostered by the Catholic faith, and which is a kind of
outward expression of the truths proclaimed by that Faith.
Catholic culture is thus an embodiment (as far as is possible) of
Catholic[2] truth in ways of thinking and acting, in the customs,
institutions and habits of our everyday lives. I do not mean only
religious (liturgical and devotional) customs and institutions. I
mean everything that goes to make up a culture. And by culture I
mean a way of life of a particular people, including everything
from when we eat our meals and how we build our houses, to
what kind of music we make and what kind of literature we
read.[3]

Our entire daily lives cannot be occupied with purely
religious practices; all of us have to eat, and most of us have and
want to do many other activities besides. So though we cannot
always be religious in this sense, we can always be Catholic,

that is, the round of our daily activities can be conducted in such a way as to express and be in harmony with our Faith. And expressing and being in harmony with the Faith can involve more than avoiding sin and exercising virtue, necessary though these are.

In education, for instance, one might think that including religion in the curriculum and having prayers and religious objects in the classroom (essential though all these are) make a school Catholic. Unfortunately they do not, for the choice of subjects, the methods used, the entire conception of what education is all about must be shaped by the Faith. Every curriculum, every set of teaching methods, make certain assumptions about what man is, what his purpose on earth is, what society is, what (if any) are the limits of its claims, etc. One cannot necessarily simply take up whatever happens to be the current curriculum and methods, add prayers and doctrine, and conclude that one has Catholic education. For the very curriculum and methods may be undermining what one is trying to inculcate in religion class.[4]

For example, when American colleges and universities abandoned the older set curriculum and seminar/recitation methods in the last quarter of the 19th century for the newer elective curriculum with lecturing as its chief teaching method and research as its goal, Catholic institutions generally adopted the new procedures, though at a slower pace.[5] Yet this largely uncritical copying of the new arrangements was not without its import for Catholic educational culture. One can argue that the changed methods were not necessarily bad in themselves, yet their wholesale acceptance as the only way of conducting higher education was inimical to what should have been the Catholic way of doing things. The elective method, for example, has destroyed the focus and unity of liberal education, making it more or less a means whereby the student prepares for his chosen career. Higher education has thereby become trivialized and its ends rendered almost wholly private, i.e., different for each individual. But a Catholic can never rightly accept the notion that the purpose of education is mostly to get a good job. Education has a purpose regardless of what we or any given student may desire. Its purpose is derived from what man is, whose nature and purpose is also independent of our thoughts and wishes. One can legitimately argue from within Catholic tradition that some student choice in curriculum is a good thing in higher education. What I take issue with is the largely unreflective change to the newer methods without asking whether and to what extent they were consonant with Catholic ideals.

To assume that educational methods are neutral is to ignore the fact that different theological and philosophical and cultural traditions give rise to different methodologies. Is it purely an accident that the emphasis on research as the goal of higher education arose in the Protestant parts of Germany? Or does it have something to do with the Protestant and secularist abandonment of the pursuit of wisdom for the pursuit of fact? The Catholic tradition in education assumed that there was a body of knowledge that was known to be both true and important, and therefore must be mastered by every student. Of course, one can argue that within this common body of knowledge there is some room for specialization and personal preference. But it is a matter of degree. The assumption behind the changed methods introduced into American institutions of higher education after 1875 was that there was no coherent body of truths necessary for everyone to know, only disparate facts, whose relative values could not be estimated, but which could be counted, described, and catalogued. This is utterly foreign to Catholic thinking. It follows, then, that if we accept electives and research into our colleges and universities, we must have a justification for them compatible with Catholic truth. We cannot simply embrace whatever secular methods are currently popular, with a presumption that no methodology is any more or less in harmony with the Faith than any other.

What is true in education is true elsewhere as well. No cultural dictate can be left unchallenged, from customs of giving birth to funeral practices, for on both of these matters, as for everything in between, the Catholic faith, if allowed to permeate and shape a society, will introduce ways of doing things consistent with and expressive of Catholic teachings on man, the family, the state, leisure, work, sex, etc. Some may respond that there is no peculiarly Catholic way to hold a fork, and that Catholic mathematics does not exist. This is certainly true, and gives the opportunity to make two distinctions. In the first place, certain things are universally true, such as Catholic theology, true philosophy, and mathematics. These are, strictly speaking, not cultural, since they should be a part of every developed culture. But in a certain sense they may be termed cultural, because, depending on whether they are present, and how they are conceived and used, they play a central role in shaping a culture. Catholic tradition does have something to say about the place of mathematics in education, for example, or the relationship between philosophy and public affairs, though neither is a matter of revelation or theology. Human life and culture must be based on truths of reason as well as of revelation. So though Catholic mathematics or physics do not exist, a true conception and use of both does, and is a necessary part of a Catholic culture. The second distinction is on the subject of the fork. Some ways of doing ordinary things, such as arranging a day as to hours for dining, sleeping, working, etc., are more in accord with Catholic ideals than others. But it does not follow from this that there is only *one* truly Catholic way. There may be several or many ways of doing some things, more or less equally in harmony with authentic Catholic life. The wonderful variety of genuine Catholic cultures is an expression of the Catholicity of the Church.[6]

Nor does this imply that only one filled with Catholic cultural ideals can be a practicing Catholic or live in a state of grace.

Everyday experience teaches us that many good Catholics steadfastly hold to all the dogmatic and moral teachings of the Church, but accept, more or less uncritically, their culture's assumptions where these are not obviously and specifically opposed to faith or morals. I think, though, that there is something lacking in their lives, for, to one degree or another, they are thwarted in outwardly expressing their faith, and hindered in living and enjoying a Catholic life.

For Catholics living in non-Catholic countries it is impossible to live a fully Catholic outward life, except perhaps as a hermit. (Consider only the difficulty of really observing a holy day, or the near impossibility of having a full-scale religious procession.) But it is possible for us to understand, to have an integral Catholic outlook. And for those Catholics living in nations of Europe or Latin America that are becoming secularized, a realization of what they are losing or about to lose may be a help to them in resolving to combat its loss. For the benefits of a Catholic culture are immense, and its loss is a disaster.

Why is an integral Catholic culture important? Primarily because man consists of both body and soul, and we may not pretend that the life our body leads is unrelated to our soul or unrelated to God. And what is true for an individual is equally true for a community.

> Nature and reason, commanding every individual devoutly to worship God in holiness (because we belong to Him and must return to Him, since from Him we came), bind also the civil community by a like law. For men living together in society, no less than individuals, are under the power of God; and society, no less than individuals, owes gratitude to God.[7]

But society's recognition of God cannot stop with worship, though obviously that is our supreme duty to Him; rather, every aspect and facet of society must be shaped or reshaped to give witness to Catholic truth. That this is the normal and natural effect of the Faith can easily be seen by looking at what we call Catholic countries. They are not Catholic simply because they contain many Catholics; they are Catholic because nearly every aspect of public and private life has been molded by the Faith. I do not mean only public or private manifestations of piety, such as processions and shrines (though these are some of the most wonderful and touching examples of the Faith in such countries), but things such as the setting of office and work hours with an eye for enhancing family life, and particularly the accepting of spiritual realities as facts of everyday life. This natural acceptance of the supernatural as real is, I think, the most distinctive mark of a thoroughly Catholic civilization. This is evidenced on both an intellectual and an ordinary plane. For if the Faith really is true, then the things it speaks of, God, Our Lady, the Angels and Saints, the Incarnation and Redemption, Heaven and Hell, are all real, as real as, and considerably more important than, the balance of payments or the GNP, and we are foolish to make decisions with consequences for our lives and our nations without thinking of these more important realities. To shut up religion in a little box and not allow it to influence important public decisions about this world is something Catholic culture will promote a wonderful mingling of things divine and things human, not because they are not distinct, but because they are both real and both ultimately from God. For since the ordinary is so obviously real, and surrounds us so much, to admit the sacred into the ordinary is to acknowledge that the sacred is real too, and not simply something reserved for special and slightly unreal occasions.

On an everyday level Catholic culture promotes the same end in a number of unexpected ways — by selling religious objects in ordinary shops, by placing holy water and shrines in public places, by being unashamed to confess that the supernatural exists and that it affects our lives. In short, by being unashamed about wanting to go to Heaven.

Because we are beings of soul and body, and because original sin has left us weak, we need all the helps we can get on our journey to Heaven. This is precisely what Catholic culture gives us. It continually reminds the forgetful that there is a God, helps the timid to have courage to think and speak of Him, assists the wavering toward virtue, and prevents us from embracing that fatal dichotomy that divides life into separate private and public spheres, mutually unaware and often operating on conflicting principles. Each of us can privately and silently dedicate his day's work to God, but when the medievals placed their craft and its guild under the protection of their patron saint, they publicly and corporately dedicated their work to God. Surely the first is as necessary as the second, but the public commitment reminds us to make the private offering. Moreover, the social nature of man and his work requires both a private and a public recognition of Christ as King, if His reign over men is to be both social and individual.

It is a commonplace that every theological heresy errs because it lacks balance. It distorts some truth or refuses to see it in its proper place, along with many other truths. Cultures do the same thing. Catholic culture puts everything into balance: the universal and the local, leisure and work, reason and emotion — all these and everything else are held in proper proportion by a Catholic culture. But any non-Catholic culture, based as it must be on an unbalanced belief, must of necessity express that imbalance in its life. Thus the very institutions of a nation, the design of its houses, the plan of its cities, will also reveal that imbalance. They overemphasize some aspects of man's nature and necessarily underemphasize others. They are the cultural heresies which are expressions of theological heresies.

We must not let anything, even the current confusion and error in the Church, prevent us from taking the time at least to understand the public and social character of the Faith. Even if right now we can rarely recover and restore a Catholic culture, we must not forget that it should exist, and that to the extent we are forced to make our Faith a merely private affair, to that extent we live impoverished Catholic lives. The norm for a Catholic is to live in a Catholic culture.

The rest of this work will explore in more detail what the characteristics of a Catholic culture are. I have deliberately omitted any systematic treatment of two important areas, politics and education, because there already are a number of works — some of which are listed in the bibliography — which give a full Catholic view of these subjects.

I will draw from the plain implications of Catholic teaching, the customs and institutions established by Catholics around the world both now and in the past, and the ideas, suggestions and hints of authors such as Belloc and Dawson who have touched upon Catholic culture in their writings. I do not insist that each and every one of my interpretations is entirely correct, but I do think that a culture such as the one I am about to sketch is the kind of civilization that our Faith demands if it is allowed free play in every area of our lives, both private and public.

NOTES

[1] "The Function of the Catholic Graduate School," *Thought* 13 (Sept. 1938), 364.

[2] Strictly speaking, Catholic culture must be based on both truths of revelation and truths of reason and experience. Some of these latter truths are so closely bound up with revealed truth, e.g., many of the major philosophical truths, that they may be termed part of the body of Catholic truths, though they are knowable by natural reason. There is another class of natural truths, however, which though equally true, is not so closely tied to Catholic theology. But many of these latter are very important as foundations for a Catholic culture, and therefore, to speak strictly, a Catholic culture would be based on both natural (or human) and Catholic truths. Among this latter class, i.e., natural truths not closely tied to revelation, are the sane and sensible ways of conducting human life and activities, from education to treatment of

the environment, which, since they are sensible, naturally characterize Catholic civilization.

[3] I am using culture in a more or less anthropological or ethnological way, as meaning (in Christopher Dawson's words) "a common way of life," the entire way of life of a particular people or civilization. Within a large common culture, such as Western culture, there may be various smaller cultural units, also called cultures. Thus we speak of French culture, Latin-American culture, etc. Both usages are appropriate, since the West does have a common way of life, based on a common heritage of ideas and institutions. Yet it is also proper to focus on the greater unity of one of the units of the civilization, and speak of French culture, or even of the culture of Provence, or what have you.

The etymology of "culture" is also very instructive as revealing quite clearly the purpose of a culture. "Culture" comes from Latin, *agri cultura*, the cultivation of a field (*ager*). Now, not everything one does to a field is *cultivation*. To throw old tin cans and dirty oil into a field will not help the crops to grow. Only the right kind of care will cause the plants to grow properly so as to become healthy food. (cf. Leo Strauss, "What is a Liberal Education?" *The College* 25 (Jan. 1974), 6-9. Not everything will cultivate man properly either. Some cultures do not perform well their function of bringing out the specific excellence of man and making him fit for both his natural and supernatural ends. I believe that Western culture, historically speaking, is the culture that best cultivates man. It combines, in Maritain's phrase, the "word of God" of Hebrew revelation with the "word of man" of Greek philosophy. Western culture, then, if it is to be true to itself, must be a Catholic culture. Otherwise, *corruptio optimi, pessima*.

[4] Fr. Bull discusses this point in the article cited above, as well as in his "The Function of the Catholic College" (New York: America Press, 1937).

[5] William T. Kane, *Catholic Library Problems* (Chicago: Loyola University Press, 1939) pp. 32-34. See also Fr. Kane's *History of Education* (Chicago: Loyola University Press, 1954) pp. 392-393.

[6] cf. my article, "The Catholicity of Catholicism," *The Wanderer* 117 (November 8, 1984).

[7] Leo XIII, Encyclical *Immortale Dei*, no. 6. Translation from *Social Wellsprings: Fourteen Epochal Documents by Pope Leo XIII* (Milwaukee: Bruce, 1940) p. 68.

1.
Economic Activity

Since the new economic usages cannot be introduced into a life attuned to the old spirit, life in general and social custom must perforce be modified, so that at no period shall social life take a course incompatible with the new criterion that informs the activity of capitalistically minded individuals.
— Amintore Fanfani[1]

What is the connection between economic activity and Catholic culture? Is there such a connection? Some might be surprised at the suggestion of a connection, for the link between them is often forgotten or ignored. But in fact a culture must have an economic base, and the economic base not only supports, but, to a great extent, shapes the resulting cultural structure. Man, of course, has power over his selection of economic ends and means. But having made his choice (or accepted unthinkingly the choices of others, living or dead) these economic ends and means have a substantial effect on his subsequent thought and life. My thesis in this chapter, then, is this: That the kind of economic activity we have, the economic arrangements we make and our attitudes toward them, have considerable effect on how we live, that is, on our culture, and tend to affect how we think about life, what we consider most important, and what sorts of motivations we consider respectable.

A good place to begin is to consider Medieval civilization in contrast to our own. Richard Tawney pointed out that the Medieval attitude toward economics and moneymaking can be summed up in the words of St. Paul, "as long as we have food and clothing let us be content with that."[2] Now these words, if taken seriously, would have a tremendous effect, not only on the life of the individual, but on the life of society. And this tremendous effect would come about because of a corollary that can be drawn from Paul's statement, namely, that economic activity has a purpose of its own.

Everything that has a purpose of its own, that is, a purpose inherent in the activity, whether or not men recognize and accept that purpose, is necessarily subject to limits, limits arising from the nature of the activity itself and its end. Eating, for example. If Socrates' dictum, that we eat to live rather than live to eat, is true, then eating has a purpose of its own. Doubtless there are gluttons who live to eat, but if eating has its own purpose, then they are simply wrong. It is not a matter of opinion, such as that Peter eats for one reason and John for another, and each is right for himself. Eating has a purpose, and the most we can hope for is to recognize and accept that purpose. Of course, this does not mean that we cannot enjoy good food, but only that our enjoyment of such food must be within the limits of eating's own purpose.[3] Otherwise we pay the price of getting sick or fat. The main point here is that although eating is something we all do, one does not have the right to ignore eating's own ends. If eating is for living, then to eat oneself to ill health or to death violates eating's own ends. No one may do this, and if one does, one will pay the penalty.

Moreover, as I said, when a thing has a purpose, it has its own limits. It is naturally subordinate to the thing for the sake of which it exists and functions; in the case of eating, living. Anything that has a purpose exists for the sake of something else, and is therefore subordinate to that something else.

All this is equally true of economic activity. It also exists for something else; thus it also has limits, and it also is subordinated to its end. What is its end? That also can be derived from St. Paul's words. The provision of "food and clothing," or, in other words, the supplying of what is needed or useful for the physical side of our lives. And the supplying of our physical needs is surely likewise for the sake of, and subordinate to, our family life and social life, our intellectual life, and our spiritual life. For we do not need houses, food, clothing, medicine, etc., as ends in themselves, but so that we can raise families, meet with our friends, educate ourselves and our children, and worship our God. Thus, just as one's eating is disordered if it defeats its end, the maintenance of life and health, so a nation's economic activity is disordered if it defeats its ultimate end, namely, the physical support of our social life, family life, intellectual life, and religious life.

Eating, though it certainly has a social side, is primarily a personal thing, and if one chooses to eat oneself to death the community as a whole will usually not suffer much.[4] Economic activity, however, though it has a personal side, has profound effects on the entire community. Whether prices rise or fall, whether there is inflation, whether interest rates are high, whether there are many jobs or few — all these are of considerable interest to the community. And because all this economic activity exists for the sake of supporting the life of the community — in individuals and families — the community has a right to some authority over the quality and type of economic activity, or else the community would be defenseless against one of its potentially most destructive enemies: disordered economic activity.

The sorts of controls over economic activity which a community directly or indirectly may rightly exercise are spelled out for us in two places: the practice of Catholic nations in the Middle Ages and later, and the teachings of the modern popes in their social encyclicals. But since this is not a work on Catholic social teaching, it is not the place to discuss these methods in detail. Instead, I will turn to the various kinds of effects economic activity can have on a community and its culture, and how this economic activity can either support or undermine the culture of the community.

If we consider the diverse types of economic activity, production, labor, distribution, lending and borrowing, etc., we can see that the quality of each type often has considerable influence on the life of a community. Thus if unemployment is high, family life is likely to deteriorate. Drunkenness, wife beating, child abuse, divorce, evictions, bankruptcies, all follow from unemployment. Low wages are often the cause of mothers working outside the home, causing increased strains on families, juvenile delinquency, etc. If interest rates are too high, then families have difficulty borrowing to buy homes, family farms often go bankrupt because of inability to meet interest payments, etc. If a factory closes, especially in a small town, the entire town may die. Neighborhoods and extended family groups will break up as the individual members seek jobs in different places. All these are obvious ways in which economic activity has a direct impact on community life. Yet, if economics exists to serve community life, then it is legitimate for the community to take steps to prevent or regulate these deleterious activities.

Economic activity, however, can also affect the social, cultural, and religious life of a people indirectly. Does the economy, for example, through production and advertising of many luxury goods, take advantage of the proclivities of our fallen nature to encourage people to spend their money, even go into debt, buying useless or harmful goods? Does it stimulate competition for the sake of competition, that is, does it encourage people who already have enough "food and clothing" to expand their businesses, compete bitterly with rivals, work long

hours, for the sake of more? Does it foster dissatisfaction with
the size of our houses and cars by inspiring envy for a higher
standard of living? Does it help people to understand the purpose of economic activity, and teach them to be satisfied if that
purpose is accomplished, or does it promote economic activity
for its own sake, or rather, for the sake of greed and restless-
ness?

If our economy does promote much restless activity, then
what effects does this have on the way people live? How does it
affect the stability of neighborhoods or of extended families? If,
for example, living near grandparents is a good thing, then does
our economic system encourage a young father to be satisfied
with a job that is merely financially satisfactory, or does it
encourage him always on to something bigger and better-
paying? Does it teach him that advancement on the job is more
important than the stability of his family and neighborhood? Or
still worse, if what is called a dynamic economy is promoted as
an unqualified blessing, then jobs are likely to move around
from place to place, necessitating moving even by those who
would prefer to stay where they are.

Does the economy make it easy for small enterprises to stay
in business, or is it mainly large firms that survive? A small or
family-run business can often be flexible and give family needs
equal place with purely economic ones, e.g., to close for lunch
or, when appropriate, to allow children to accompany or help
their parents in their work. A large firm can do few or none of
these kinds of things, and it can more easily schedule people to
work the lunch hour, thus destroying a potentially common
family meal.

These examples show some of the ways, both direct and
indirect, that the quality of economic activity in a nation influences its life. The root problem is that when a nation's
economic life is disordered in the ways explained above, the that
nation's people has forgotten that economic activity has a pur-

pose of its own, regardless of the personal motives or desires of any individual. Even if every man in a particular country believed that the purpose of economic activity was to make as much money as possible, that would not change its purpose, just as if everyone thought that the purpose of eating was to endlessly gratify the palate, that would not change the inherent end of eating. What therefore is to be done?

First, two related truths must be realized: That ideas ultimately determine conduct, and that man has free will. As Hilaire Belloc liked to point out, modern writers talk about "trends" and "forces" and "the state of the economy" as if they were active agents and the real movers of men. As in "Trends force us to act in such a way . . . " or "The state of the economy obliges us to . . . ." Not true. As Belloc said, these kinds of statements are signs of our practical materialism. Human beings are free, and, depending on what decisions they make, can decide to do anything humanly possible. Of course, man cannot make bricks if there is no straw, but the range of choices possible for us is much wider than most men realize. And the choices we make depend largely on what we believe about the ultimate things, what we believe is important. Our economic system, which values families so low, did not come into being by itself. It came into being because of ideas, ideas which influenced those with power enough to persuade or force everyone else to accept the new system. It is neither inevitable nor natural.

If we admit that certain ways of living are better than others, that is, that certain cultural arrangements are better than others, and that an economic system can affect these ways of living, then what can be done about such an economic system that is not serving its end of supporting the culture very well? First, as I said above, we must be convinced of what is right, and convinced that we can do something about it. Then we have to know what to do. Most forms of socialism were originally attempts to establish an economic system that was supportive of certain human values, but they all founder on either materialism or collectivism or both. On the other hand, the claim that is commonly made for free market capitalism, namely, that if the government lets the economy alone things will turn out best for everyone, is also inadmissible, as both history and papal authority testify.[5] Therefore, we need to understand the spirit in which Medieval Catholic culture and the papal teachings regard the economic order.

First of all, harmony is the most prominent note in this Catholic attitude. God's creation, though marred by the Fall, is still essentially good, and therefore there is no necessary conflict among the various elements in the social or economic orders, labor and capital, producers and consumers, rural and urban dwellers, or even among producers or vendors of the same product.[6] All need each other, and this need does not require any one group to exploit any other. To make use of our neighbor's labor is not exploitation, if the neighbor receives his due in return.

The second major concept found in Catholic teaching is that of reasonableness. A worker, the popes teach, needs a living wage because he must live and must support his family. It is unreasonable for him to receive anything less, because man has a duty to preserve his life, and a workingman has no means other than his labor to provide for his and his family's needs.[7] If he cannot earn enough by means of his daily work, where else is he to get it? By working nights too?

Just as a wage earner deserves what is reasonable, so do others. The medievals, for example, conceived that a craftsman deserved the opportunity of providing through his work for his and his family's reasonable standard of living, but it was not considered reasonable for him to expand his business and drive his fellow craftsmen into ruin. A man deserved one living, not two or three, even if he were clever or unscrupulous enough to accumulate two or three or more. As Chesterton said, to limit the amount of property a man may have is no more to attack the institution of private property than to limit the number of wives a man may have is to attack the institution of marriage. It is not that no man can be rich or that all must have the same amount; rather that no man can reasonably expect the opportunity to make more than a decent living, since society will suffer by the striving, the fierce competition, the bankruptcies, strikes, layoffs, etc., that invariably accompany an economy in which men are permitted to strive for as much as and anything they want. If a man can become rich without engaging in practices which are harmful to others, without disturbing the health or stability of the social order, then the community should not hinder him. But if economic activity has a purpose, then it is unreasonable for anyone to resent society having regulations to foster and protect this purpose, especially since violation of the purpose results in social upheaval. It is just as unreasonable for someone to resent society having regulations forbidding adultery or homosexual activity. An individual might claim that for him sex has no other purpose than pleasure, but that does not change the facts. Sex has a purpose of its own, regardless of any personal inclinations or opinions. We are not reasonable if we expect society to adjust its institutions and laws to permit us to indulge ourselves unchecked by consideration for others. This is as true in economics as it is in sex. We cannot expect more than what is reasonable, and if we think the purpose of economics is opportunity for limitless gain, then society has the right to restrain us, just as it may do with the man who thinks the purpose of sex is limitless irresponsible pleasure. A problem arises only if the community via the state authorities goes about defending itself from greed or lust in a way that brings about some greater evil, as statism or socialism do with economics, and as (for example) placing a policeman in every bedroom or motel would do with sex.

The thing to be desired, therefore, is that everyone in the community be persuaded that economics has a purpose, and that it is a part of the hierarchical order of human activities, the lower serving the higher. One of the earliest and greatest defections from Christian morality and truth by modern man was the setting up of economics as an autonomous activity within human society, no longer serving the common good, but existing for whatever private ends each individual invested it with. Of course, according to Adam Smith, this totality of private ends was somehow going to serve the common good, but it is odd that every other human activity is thought to need intelligent direction and control, the only exception being the free play of greed and monetary gain. Pius XI makes it clear that this is not the Catholic attitude:

> Just as the unity of human society cannot be built upon "class" conflict, so the proper ordering of economic affairs cannot be left to the free play of rugged competition. From this source, as from a polluted spring, have proceeded all the errors of the "individualistic" school. This school, forgetful or ignorant of the social and moral aspects of economic activities, regarded these as completely free and immune from any intervention by public authority, for they would have in the market place and in unregulated competition a principle of self-direction more suitable for guiding them than any created intellect which might intervene.[8]

Our Medieval ancestors showed us the right path, when they subordinated economic activity to the "created intellect" of the guilds for the sake of the common good, not in a statist or socialist manner, but in a fashion consonant with legitimate human freedom and prosperity. We have gone so far in the opposite direction that large corporations openly justify selling technical equipment and processes to the communists for the sake of gain, evidently unconcerned with the fact that they thus support the plans for conquest by our chief human enemies, not to mention the oppression of the nations already ground under the Soviet heel. But if the pursuit of the almighty dollar is judged superior even to our national security, how can we possibly convince them that such seemingly trivial matters as the welfare of our families and the stability of our neighborhoods are more important than more money? We cannot convince them, the owners and directors of wealth, because we have not yet convinced ourselves. Our chief problem is that our culture is not subordinate to Catholic teaching about materialism, the pursuit of wealth, the place of the family, etc. We do not listen to the voices of the supreme pontiffs, the record of Catholic history, and the opinions of nearly all authentic expounders of Catholic traditions in our time, such as Chesterton, Belloc or Christopher Dawson. Instead we see how far we can justify our present ways of living and thinking without obviously violating any explicit papal condemnation.

Under our present system we put man and the things necessary for man, the worship of God, the family, even material prosperity itself, in a less important place than the freedom to seek private gain regardless of the unsettling consequences on the community. A restoration of Catholic culture must have as one of its first concerns the creation of a proper attitude toward the place of economic activity in a nation, with a firm resolve to use every legitimate means to confine it to that place, avoiding at the same time both statism and socialism. If the role of economics in restoring Christian culture is neglected on the grounds that something so material has nothing to do with culture, or because of complacent acceptance of the modern outlook, then no lasting renewal can come about, either in society or within our own minds.

NOTES

[1] *Catholicism, Protestantism and Capitalism* (New York: Sheed & Ward, 1939) p. 45.

[2] I Timothy 6:8. Jerusalem Bible.

[3] Nourishment obviously need not be foremost in our minds when we eat or prepare food, but it must govern our choice of food in a general way. A particular meal or day's food may be chosen with no regard for nutrition or health, but we cannot always do this, or sickness will result. Of course, within the broad limits imposed by nourishment we seek the kind and amount of food that we like, but still within those limits, however broad they may be.

[4] Nevertheless we have — or had until recently — laws against suicide, a fact that proves Christian civilization did not regard the individual as autonomous or devoid of duties to his fellows.

[5] cf. Encyclical *Quadragesimo Anno*, nos. 88 and 107.

[6] We naively assume that two merchants selling the same item must be in competition with each other. But two physicians in the same town do not regard each other as "the competition," and look for the first opportunity of underselling, or somehow putting the other out of business. Presumably, if there was not enough work in one locale for two doctors, one already there might resent the arrival of another. But not because he wanted to compete; only because he expected to make a reasonable living by his practice. Why should those who sell bread or milk or shoes not do the same? cf. Richard Tawney's excellent discussion of this matter in *The Acquisitive Society* (New York: Harcourt, Brace & World, 1948) pp. 91-122, especially pp. 95-96.

[7] cf. Encyclical *Rerum Novarum*, no. 34.

[8] Encyclical *Quadragesimo Anno*, no. 88. Translation from *Seven Great Encyclicals* (New York: Paulist, 1963) pp. 149-150.

2.
Technology

. . . the Faith would never have produced Huddersfield or Pittsburg.

— Hilaire Belloc[1]

In discussing the cultural effects of technology two extremes must be avoided. One is to blindly welcome every new invention, regardless of whether and how it benefits mankind, as an example of the fulfillment of God's command, "Conquer the earth"[2] or as a working out of human development and achievement. This naive attitude toward technology is the ally of the creation of many unnecessary or even entirely useless or harmful goods. The other extreme is typified by the Old Order Amish. They very correctly insist on the primacy of the spiritual and the cultural, and have made the judgment that technological progress must be completely halted if their culture with its spiritual values is to be preserved. At first glance it might seem as if they were right, since innovation would probably mean the end of the Amish way of life. But what is wrong with thus freezing technology in the 16th century is that genuinely human technological advances serve rather than undermine culture. I will argue below that our present attitudes toward technology are radically flawed, but both technology and technological development in themselves are good and are meant to serve humanity. There is no logical reason why the Amish have chosen the level of the 16th century at which to stop technology; they might as well have chosen the 4th, the 12th or the 20th. It was only by an historical accident that their community came into being in the 16th century, and their leaders apparently have felt that it is better to freeze technology than to jeopardize the community's stability.[3] This is, in the true sense of the word, a conservative judgment, and shows very clearly why some principle more than mere conservation must regulate and inspire human thought and action. Although the Amish can see all around them the corrosive effects of unrestrained technology, a consideration of life even in a primitive community will demonstrate that technology as such is truly beneficial to mankind. For every society uses some technology, and were we to employ none at all we would be reduced to going naked, living in caves, eating wild plants and raw meat, and drinking water from our cupped hands. No reasonable person will defend such an existence as proper for human beings, so therefore the question becomes how much technology and of what sort. Not all examples of technology need be good, simply because technology in itself is good. For though all things natural to human beings are good when used for the purposes for which they were intended, they are often used for other purposes as well — perhaps more times than not. So though the thing or activity may be perfectly good and laudable in itself, most of its manifestations may be bad and harmful. Therefore it would be quite reasonable to be a friend of technology and yet opposed to very many individual instances of it.

Next a very important point needs to be clarified since its very opposite is often asserted as an obvious truth. The point is simply this: It is not true to say that all technology is neutral and that it is only in the use or misuse of an object that good or evil lies. Of course there is some truth in this. A hammer can be used to build a house or kill one's grandmother. In neither case is the hammer to be praised or blamed, only the human actor. Secondly, it is true that, strictly speaking, no invention whatever is morally good or bad; only persons are moral agents. But admitting all this, I still assert: Technology is not necessarily neutral. And the reason for this is simple: Certain inventions, given our fallen natures, are just too much of a temptation for us. They invite, so to speak, their misuse, or rather their use in such a way that the effects on the life of man in society — for whose sake all technology exists — are harmful. And there are, or at least could be, some inventions that have no proper use; to use one at all is to commit a wrong. Let us take up these two cases separately.

The first is that of inventions whose use, especially on a large scale, results in social evils. Moreover, there need be nothing sinful about any individual use of such an invention, only that widespread use in some way injures society. But it is man's fallen state that, acting on the invention, brings about the injury. The invention in itself does not demand it. Why, then, attribute evil to the machine? Only because the invention is the occasion and necessary condition for some disruption of society, a disruption that is an evil, and thus, the invention may likewise be termed an evil. Given our human weaknesses, our propensity toward unnecessary luxuries, our tendency to take the path of least resistance, our habitual disinclination to follow the better part, our shortsightedness, and our failure to see the consequences of our actions, the proposition that technology is always neutral is not tenable. We call something bad if it fails to fulfill or contribute toward its end very well. This is true of the technology I am speaking of, for because of our fallen state, this kind of technology does not contribute well to its end of serving mankind. For prudence surely commands us in all that we do to take account of reality, of what is, among which things man's wounded nature must surely take one of the first places. Thus we cannot consider those things which are occasions of cultural disturbance to be mere indifferent factors in the act.

Certainly, though, if the specific difficulty the invention was created to overcome is important enough, and its negative impact slight or otherwise unimportant, this would change our evaluation. It will be a question of practical wisdom each time to judge whether a disruptive technology justifies itself suf-ficiently by its contribution to human welfare, or whether it serves a part at the expense of the whole. The major problem does not lie in the difficulty of making such judgments; rather in getting men to admit that inventions with negative impacts on human life need to justify themselves.

The second kind of invention I distinguished above is that which has no licit use at all. For example, a bomb whose only use was to destroy entire cities, a newly-refined means of performing abortions, a device for making poisoned toys. No one of these has any legitimate use, and to manufacture any one of them is to invite wrongdoing. It is still true, of course, that men have to choose to use such things, but it is rather silly to suggest they would be produced just to be gazed at.

Of course, I am predicating good and evil of machines and gadgets in an analogical sense, but, I maintain, in a legitimate one. We call arrangements good or bad insofar as they make it easy or difficult for men to accomplish some end. Similarly I call technological mechanisms good or bad as they fulfill the purposes of technology well or ill. If an invention truly serves human culture, then it is good; if it does not, or if it serves it in only some narrow aspect, to the injury of the whole, then, probably, it is bad. For even though men are responsible for the acts that lead to such damage, if we are prudent, we will anticipate and make allowance for our wounded natures, not create temptations we foresee cannot be handled.

To sum up what I have said so far: Technology and its continuing development are good if they further the ends of civilization; if not, then they are bad. Furthermore, this depends not simply on human transgressions, because some inventions themselves are bad, either because they have no right use, or because they are certain to cause harm with no corresponding benefit to offset the damage they do. Next I will discuss more closely ways in which disruptive technology can injure a culture, and what I consider the fundamental error of our present unsound attitude toward technology.

If what has just been said is true, then technology disrupts culture whenever it makes it easy or encourages one to do acts which, instead of building up the culture and serving the ends of man, serve various short term interests, either sinful as such, or not sinful, but nevertheless contrary to the common good. Moreover, this can be true of devices which serve legitimate though narrow ends, namely for the right living of individuals, families and communities in society, which in turn is to serve the eternal salvation of the individuals involved, part of "the universal teleological order" through which "we shall be led by progressive stages to the final end of all, God Himself, our highest and lasting good."[4] The place of technology in this is to make easier the acquisition of certain material goods for the satisfaction of the needs of our cultural, social, intellectual and spiritual lives. Thus technology can fail in its mission not only by neglecting to provide these material goods, but also by doing so in a way which undermines that for which they exist, man's life in society and culture.

For example, it is a principle of Catholic social thought that widespread ownership of productive property is a good thing, promoting a healthy kind of self-reliance, allowing a family to provide for its needs, encouraging the responsible and equitable distribution of the goods of the earth, fostering stability in the community, and furthering the production of useful material goods, for "men always work harder and more readily when they work on that which is their own."[5] The most obvious kind of productive property is farmland, as Pius XII said, "none is more conformable to nature than the land, the holding on which the family lives, and from the products of which it draws all or part of its subsistence."[6] Family farms promote wise and careful use of the soil, for the farmer realizes he and his family must draw an entire lifelong subsistence from his farm, and cannot exploit the soil for quick profit and move on to another place. They likewise give farmers and their families a dignity they would never know as hired laborers, and give to society a stable base.[7] What does technology have to do with this? Agricultural technology can be designed and invented which enhances small farming or which makes it very difficult for small farmers to survive. Certain very large machines for harvesting, etc., expensive to buy and to operate, can hardly be afforded by small farmers. Thus these farmers are put in a very difficult competitive position vis-à-vis large corporate "farmers," who can easily afford such machines. This is one of the things that has led to the decrease in the number of small farms and the consequent death of rural culture. For when families live on the land, they have all the needs, cultural, economic and social, of families. They require churches, schools, stores, post offices, etc., located at convenient distances. And these institutions naturally spring up since there are families with permanent needs who will patronize them. Thus the economic and social base of farming towns and villages is preserved. But now we have increasingly large farms, highly mechanized, with few people actually living on the farm. Moreover, these few, mostly hired laborers, cannot have the same interest in creating a true rural culture, because they do not expect to spend their entire lives there, and generally do not have families. Thus small towns and villages die as they lose their economic and cultural base, and people drift into the large cities, creating gigantic concentrations of men, much bigger than cities were ever intended to become.[8]

If we care about preserving family farms and preventing the depopulation of the countryside, then the question of agricultural technology is important. We cannot dismiss it as merely a technical matter. Its direct influence on the kind and quality of life in our society is evident.

One way, then, in which technology can harm society is by fostering bigness for the sake of bigness. It usually does this without asking whether the new technology is needed or useful, whether there is anything wrong with the present arrangement, or whether the altered state of affairs will be, on balance, better or worse. Which brings me to the root problem with our present attitudes toward technology. We see a problem to be solved: how to make a certain process faster or cheaper or more efficient or whatever. We concentrate on solving that one problem, but we never stop to ask what consequences will follow from our solution. What its effect on the whole will be. We have isolated one single aspect of a complex and interrelated unity, and changed that one aspect without consideration of any other facet. We have, for example, figured out how to get from point A to point B very fast. But why we want to go from A to B, whether it will contribute to a better life in general for people to go from A to B faster, whether there was any sort of benefit to going slowly from A to B — none of these questions did we think worth considering. In the past men could travel as far as they wanted to — if they really wanted to. Now one just thoughtlessly jumps into a car and goes. We have made it easy for families and communities to be broken up, for rural areas to lose most of their economic base and institutions — churches, schools, stores, post offices — because it is now easy to drive to the next big town. How can we expect the government to keep open a post office in a small village when we demonstrate by our driving habits that we are quite willing to drive 10 or 20 miles for a pack of cigarettes? How can we consistently oppose the closing of a small country parish if we regularly drive to the large city for our recreation? When, in creating our modern means of transportation, did we ever face up to questions such as: Do we really want neighborhood stores to close? Do we really want local and family recreational activities to cease? Do we really want each family member to go his separate way of an evening? We assumed the new inventions were good because we assumed getting from A to B faster was a good. An unqualified good. Perhaps in a prelapsarian state it would be. But given the fact that man has fallen, and is likely to take the path of least resistance, how could we have expected these new means of transportation not to affect society? And if society is of more value than technology, then how could we possibly have admitted these inventions without in the least examining their probable effects? We did it surely because of our purely quantified outlook on things. We can quantify the distance and length of time involved between A and B; we can quantify the cost per unit of production; we can quantify the speed at which we make each unit. So we speed up, we reduce the cost — all things we can quantify and thus approve of — with absolutely no thought of their consequences.

The origins of this point of view are to be found in such early modern philosophers as Francis Bacon and René Descartes, who were writing at the very time modern science and technology were developing. Indeed, modern science is almost purely a technological science, interested not in knowing but in doing, in obtaining results.[9] As such, it tends to regard every technological advance as a good. It has a kind of habitual outlook or assumption which does not even think to ask the question: Is it possible that some new technological discovery might be harmful to mankind? As soon as the question is asked, one is aware that the answer is not obviously a No. We must admit at least the possibility that some inventions do not really serve humanity, unless we hold for some kind of technological determinism, with some invisible hand working everything out for our benefit.

A technology, therefore, that truly served mankind, would be one in which men clearly realized that each invention had to not only make some one particular process easier or cheaper, but at the same time not disrupt or corrupt any important human activity or cultural value. I doubt whether most inventors think much about whether they are benefiting their fellow men. I suspect their attention is focused on the technological puzzle before them, necessarily reduced to some narrow and quantified problem.

Additionally, as Fanfani notes,[10] our economic system has acted as a powerful stimulus for technological innovation, with the great cost of the innovations themselves making for even more economic striving, as their owners sought to minimize risks and cover their new capital costs. Thus these two forces, both often socially disruptive, have fed each other throughout modern times, as they still do.

In spite of all this, it should be clear from what I have said that I think one can be a friend of technology and yet suspicious of, or opposed to, much of the technology around us. This might seem a paradoxical conclusion to some, but only because the connection between technology and culture, like that between economic activity and culture, is not often recognized. But it is nevertheless very important. Our patterns of entertainment and socializing, the extent to which families move about, the kinds of work we do and the arrangements of property ownership that we have — in all these matters the technology of the society is among the most important determining factors. Thus if society realizes the extent to which stability contributes to such important concerns as preservation of traditional customs, stability in families, contentedness with one's place in life, with the consequences of domestic and civic peace, respect between generations, and many other values, then it is likely to view too much and too sudden technological innovation as detrimental to the health of the community. Unless technological change is an end in itself, then it must be subordinated to civil and domestic happiness, gibes about living in a backward culture notwithstanding. Probably, though, there is room for unlimited technological improvement, provided that it is slow and always subordinated to the real needs and welfare of mankind.

What can a civilization do in order to control technology and make it a servant instead of a master? The most necessary thing is to change our attitude toward science and technology, and to remove the spur that our economy gives to wholesale innovation. As far as science is concerned, we must remember that science means knowledge, and that the noblest kind of knowledge is its own end. Bacon said that knowledge was power, and scientific knowledge has certainly proved itself powerful. But power is not its end. That is not what it is for. Without questioning the need for applied science, I nonetheless deny that the present nearly exclusive orientation of our scientific research toward ultimate technological application is right.[11] There is something more noble than better gadgets. At the same time, since we really do need technology, we must make sure that it is always an aid for human life. At present it sometimes is this, but it is just as likely to undermine human society, and by our present criteria we cannot distinguish a good invention that serves man from a bad one that harms him, even if it may make easier some small facet of life. A few concrete things can be done, however, such as a repeal of the patent laws in order to remove an artificial stimulus to innovation. True humane technological progress must continue, but our present patent laws encourage indiscriminate innovation and discourage stability. In the long run, though, society will have to rely mainly on the diffusion of a true Catholic attitude among its members,[12] and, in exceptional cases, on governmental action to ban particularly harmful inventions.

If the world's activity exists for the sake of human social, intellectual, cultural and spiritual life, then technology too must be curbed, and oriented once again toward its proper end, the serving of man's material needs, without disruption of his purposes and higher life.[13]

NOTES

[1] "The Faith and Industrial Capitalism" in *Essays of a Catholic Layman in England* (New York: Macmillan, 1931) p. 39.

[2] cf. Genesis 1:28. Jerusalem Bible.

[3] Actually the Amish attitude toward technology, and the reasons for their attitude, are more complex than implied here. They have not in every case refused to use more recent technology.

[4] Encyclical *Quadragesimo Anno*, no. 43. Translation from *Seven Great Encyclicals* (New York: Paulist, 1963) p. 136.

[5] Encyclical *Rerum Novarum*, no. 35. Translation from *Seven Great Encyclicals*, p. 22.

[6] Quoted in Benjamin L. Masse, *Justice for All* (Milwaukee: Bruce, 1964) p. 129.

[7] Compare the following discussion of Pius XII's statements about the value of farming and rural life, and technological and economic threats to its continued existence:

> Later on in his pontificate, the Pope grew concerned over the use of capitalistic techniques in agriculture. He conceded that these had expanded farm production, but he was fearful that they might alter the character of rural living by making the countryside a mere expansion of the city. Marxism, with its "idolatrous worship of technology and industrialization," professedly aims at this goal, he said, so that the countryside is "reduced to nothing more than a reserve of manpower for industrial production." But economic liberalism, "once the pursuit of gain on the part of finance capitalism bears with all its weight upon economic life," also brings about the same result. Because of the spiritual, as well as economic, values inherent in work in the fields, the Pope insisted that farm technology be subordinated to man (To the International Catholic Congress on Rural Problems, July 2, 1951). In his view, "keeping within the spirit of the social doctrine of the Church," farming is more than an economic activity aimed at making a profit; it is a noble way of life eminently suited to strengthen the family — a "bulwark of sound liberty, a protective dike against the danger of urbanism, and an effective contribution to the continuation of the sound traditions of the people" (Address on Problems of Rural Life, September 18, 1957). Benjamin L. Masse, *Justice for All*, p. 130.

[8] cf. Christopher Dawson, "The Evolution of the Modern City" in *The Dynamics of World History* (New York: New American Library, 1962) pp. 189-198.

[9] cf. C.S. Lewis, *The Abolition of Man* (New York: Macmillan, 1965) pp. 86-91.

[10] *Catholicism, Protestantism and Capitalism* (New York: Sheed & Ward, 1939) pp. 140-141, 174-175, 182.

[11] It is, however, questionable whether any of the scientific research presently being carried on could be reoriented toward speculative knowledge, i.e., knowledge for its own sake. It would probably have to be a very different kind of research, though perhaps using much of the same equipment.

[12] cf. Amintore Fanfani, *Catholicism, Protestantism and Capitalism*, p. 141. Sumptuary laws, however, which limited and regulated what luxuries people could possess, are entirely traditional within Catholic civilization. They might well be revived.

[13] The question of industrial innovation must also be touched on, since it is one of the most common causes of industrial instability, resulting in loss of jobs and layoffs, forced relocation of people, plant closings, and so forth. It has the same causes as more general technological innovation, except that here the economic pressures operate more directly. Unfortunately one country, to say nothing of one industry or factory, cannot successfully address the problem alone. To the extent that nations comprise one world economy, cooperation in a new approach to technology is needed. In spite of this difficulty, the existence of the problem must be recognized, even if it cannot presently be dealt with.

3.
Culture in the Narrow Sense

Throughout this book my concern is with culture in the broad sense, as meaning the entire way of life and thought of a people, but in this chapter I will be concerned with culture in its narrow and perhaps more usual sense, that is, with the arts, literature, music, etc.

First, to make a number of divisions and definitions. Using culture in its broad sense, there are two types of culture, educated culture and folk culture. Educated culture is that culture which exists in the centers of a high or advanced civilization, and uses all the resources of that civilization for investigation of truth, basing its cultural practices — in medicine, education, the arts, or whatever — more on discovery, or presumed discovery, of truth than on simple tradition. Urban areas are typically part of an educated culture.

Folk culture, on the other hand, is a culture handed down within a group which has little or no contact with the patterns of living and thinking of an educated culture, and whose basis for cultural practices is largely tradition, or "how it's always been done." This is not to say that the cultural traditions can never have a rational basis, but simply that it is not the rational basis that is the major factor in the retention of the practice.

A folk culture can exist either by itself, as in the case of a primitive culture, or it can exist on the fringes of, and as a part of the same civilization as an educated culture. Western civilization today is entirely or almost entirely an educated culture in

Europe and North America, but in Latin America there are areas in which folk culture predominates or has much influence. But in the United States of a hundred years ago Appalachia was in large part a folk culture, and in past centuries in Europe rural and mountainous areas often contained folk cultures. The accounts by Johnson and Boswell of their journey from the educated culture of 18th-century London and Edinburgh to the Highlands and Hebrides of Scotland well illustrates the coexistence within the same civilization of both educated and folk cultures.

Except for a primitive society, there is no pure folk culture, since influences from the educated culture continually affect a folk society, just as within an educated culture elements of a folk cultural approach can often be found. It is rather a question of which influences predominate, especially if one set of influences is almost exclusively dominant.

Within any culture, folk or educated, there will be many practices concerned with everyday living, kind of medical care, type of education, material objects used, and the like. There will also be those practices and customs I call cultural in the narrow sense, art, music, literature, etc. In a folk culture these latter will of course partake of the same folk character as the everyday customs, and thus we have folk music, folk art, and so forth. But in an educated culture things are more complicated. Because of the complexity of the culture, there is a horizontal division, as it were, between "highbrow" or high culture and "lowbrow" culture. High culture is simply those cultural activities (in the narrow sense of culture) associated with, and under the care or influence of, the institutions in the society explicitly charged with care of the arts and literature, such as, in our times, museums, symphony orchestras, literary and intellectual journals and societies, colleges and universities, and the like. Considering, for example, the manifold forms of classical music produced in the past and now, the best definition we can give of classical music is "that music associated with certain cultural institutions, such as the court, the Church, the academy, etc." I do not see any other way, e.g., any strictly musical way, of noting any similarity between Bach and the electronic music of a John Cage, except to note the similar connection each had with the recognized cultural institutions of its day. Thus I define all high culture in what might be called a sociological fashion.

"Lowbrow" culture, on the other hand, is simply all other cultural (narrow sense) activity taking place in the educated part of the civilization. But this can be of more than one sort. One type, widely prevalent today, is mass culture. As I use the term, mass culture means not any culture that the mass of the people has, but mass-produced culture, music, art, literature, that is produced only or mainly with an eye for gain, and with little or no regard for the intrinsic ends of the arts. It is market-oriented art, and has elevated an extrinsic purpose (gain) to be its final cause.[1] Since gain is its end, it is necessarily distributed over as wide an area as possible to take advantage of a bigger market. It is likewise uniform in form or appearance to cut production costs, i.e., the exact same picture or recorded song is sold in as wide an area as possible. Only in this way can the monetary benefits of the large market be realized.

What is the alternative to mass culture? It is an amalgam made up of elements of high culture and elements of folk culture, which I will here call popular culture. A popular culture differs from a mass culture in two important ways: in its connection with high culture and in its causes and manner of dissemination.

Regarding high culture, a popular culture is connected with a high culture, and vice versa, in that both propose the same cultural ends and employ the same canons of taste, but in different ways or degrees. That is, what each teaches and the way in which each entertains or delights is analogous to the way the other does these things. They may even make use of the same cultural objects, but again, in not exactly the same way.

For example, before its suppression by the Puritans in 1642,
English drama was remarkable because of its appeal to all
classes of the population, learned and unlearned. From the
church plays of the Middle Ages to those of Shakespeare and his
immediate successors, these plays were liked by all, because the
unity that then existed within that civilization was such that the
same cultural ends were appreciated by all. But although *Ham-
let* is one work of literature, there are different elements in it,
from high and sublime soliloquies to slapstick and melodrama.
That is, it contains both high and popular cultural features. In
fact, these seemingly disparate features are characteristic of
English drama before 1642, and though different groups in the
audience may have focused on different aspects of the play, yet
it was still the same play they were watching, and basically the
same point each absorbed.[2] How different it is today when a vast
gulf separates the products of high culture from the concoctions
of mass culture, and the popular nature of Shakespeare's plays is
obscured and forgotten. One need not go as far as the old
dramatists did to have a unity between high and popular culture
— a unity, by the way, beneficial not only to the popular culture
but to the high culture as well, for it helps prevent artificiality
and superficiality in it. Contemporary high culture suffers from
the fact that no one really *likes* it; one reads or listens or views
because one wants to be *au courant*, a real perversion of the
purposes of art. Contemporary creators of high culture in our
civilization (as distinguished from those who perform or exhibit
high cultural works from the past) live in a little world cut off
from ordinary life and from their fellows, surviving only because they themselves define what is good contemporary art or
music, and those anxious to be approved and considered cul-
tured do not dispute their judgments. Business corporations and
governments are regularly duped by this small group of creators
of modern art, music, and literature into subsidizing idiotic
sculptures and musical works which offend the eyes or ears of

everyone, but are considered "serious" and "worthwhile" just because the little group that surrounds their creators says they are.

The other way in which mass culture differs from popular culture is in the motives of those who produce it and in its resulting means of distribution, what I referred to above as its causes and manner of dissemination. And because of these differences, popular culture possesses something that mass culture does not, namely variety. Because lack of variety is something characteristic of modern culture in both the broad and narrow senses, a discussion of the importance of variety will not be out of place.

Variety is important, I think, more as evidence of something else than as something valuable in its own right. Variety is important because it is evidence of local autonomy or control, and local autonomy is important because man as creator is important. The popes teach, for example, that when men own the property on which they work, good things usually result. Leo XIII stated this beautifully in speaking of farm land:

> Men always work harder and more readily when they work on that which is their own; nay, they learn to love the very soil which yields in response to the labor of their hands, not only food to eat, but an abundance of the good things for themselves and those that are dear to them.[3]

The same is true, *mutatis mutandis*, of other kinds of property and labor. The artisan in his own workshop works with pride using his own tools for the benefit of himself and his family. He can see the productions of his own hands taking shape before him. No employee, especially of a large concern, could possibly take the same joy in his work as can one working on and with his own property. This is simply an example of the principle of subsidiarity, that

one should not withdraw from individuals and commit to the
community what they can accomplish by their own enterprise
and industry. So, too, it is an injustice and at the same time a
grave evil and a disturbance of right order, to transfer to the
larger and higher collectivity functions which can be performed and provided for by lesser and subordinate bodies.[4]

If an individual can perform efficiently in his own workshop or
on his own farm, then it is wrong and disturbing to the social
order to commit the matter to some large factory or corporate
farm, or to a Communist collective farm. The same is true for
political organization and also for cultural (in the narrow sense)
creation. That is, if individual localities can create their own art
and music and dance, then it is "a disturbance of right order, to
transfer to the larger and higher collectivity" these tasks, such as
a radio station beaming its music over wide areas, a record
company selling its recorded music throughout entire nations,
and so on, for recorded music is surely responsible for the
practical disappearance of musicmaking at the family and
neighborhood levels. Thus variety is important because it is
evidence that cultural creation is in the hands of those it should
be in, namely local communities, neighborhoods, and families.
This is not to extol variety or newness for its own sake, for in fact
local cultural creations are likely to be variations on a larger
common culture, as for example, the many local variants of
individual folk songs that formerly could be found throughout
the United States. These versions were all related, but differed
from one another according to local adaptations and traditions.
Such local variations, customs, and traditions, whether in music
and the arts, in cookery, in patterns of speech, all were evidence
that "larger and higher" organizations had not yet arrogated to
themselves tasks which were being satisfactorily performed by
"lesser and subordinate bodies."

Variety, then, is a sign that local control of culture has not
been done away with for the sake of the gains that come from a

larger market. Popular culture is marked by such variety because it is not created and propagated solely for the sake of gain. This is not to say that a musician or artist in a popular culture did not expect to make a living by his art. He may well have expected it, but the difference between him and the controllers of mass culture is that the latter see the art as only an incidental and convenient means to the end of moneymaking, while the former, no matter how rich he might have desired to become, still considered himself as an artist.[5] He hoped to live by his art and perhaps even become rich, but never regarded the art as merely a handy method of making money, a method that could be exchanged with no regrets next week if selling used cars or vacuum cleaners seemed likely to be more profitable.

Most men's motives are mixed, and very often there is nothing especially to be deplored about that fact. I do not claim that the creators of popular or folk culture are especially single-hearted or pure, only that because the dominant economic ideas in their societies had not taught them that maximization of profits was not only legitimate but praiseworthy, they were usually content with the customary rewards and returns incidental to their professions. They saw their individual arts as parts of a culture and as occupying a distinct and recognized place within that culture. The idea had not occurred to them (and in truth they usually lacked the technological means) of extending their particular art or skill over as wide an area as possible and to as many people as possible, regardless of what effects this would have on those other areas and peoples, all for the sake of money and more money.

A practitioner of the arts in a popular culture has regard for his own art, however highly he may at the same time regard money. The propagators of mass culture would propagate absolutely anything at all if they thought it would sell and would not get them into legal trouble. Therefore, because of its seeking ever wider markets for its products, the means of dissemination of mass culture are also necessarily different from those of popular culture.

The legitimate means of cultural dissemination within a popular culture are all those that are in harmony with the principle of subsidiarity. If, for example, popular music over the radio is found to interfere with the control of culture by lower and smaller bodies and regions, then this mode of cultural propagation is not admissible, not because there is anything wrong with the radio as such, but because it is not compatible with the fundamental principle of both social and cultural life, subsidiarity. Mass culture, of course, seeks the widest dissemination possible, but what means will popular culture use? Primarily those which allow a natural diffusion of culture, the kind of diffusion which accompanies natural contacts among people, such as family gatherings, dances, fairs, picnics, church suppers, and whatever local entertainments are traditional in an area. Again, this is because only such means of cultural diffusion do not violate the principle of subsidiarity. The electronic media may have a place in the diffusion of high culture and of intellectual works such as lectures, but they definitely will destroy genuine popular culture and so must not be permitted to function in that area. People have a natural desire to hear and create music and art, and if the instruments of mass culture are silenced, then a renaissance of popular culture will occur. Perhaps not a splendid renaissance, especially at first, but still one that respects the right of "lesser and subordinate bodies" to create and live in their own cultures, not simply absorb and conform to someone else's conceptions, still less when that someone else has really no interest in culture or in the people for whom his products are intended.

Among a people thoroughly imbued with a Catholic sense, this popular culture that will arise, more or less spontaneously, when mass culture has been overthrown, will certainly be Catholic. But it is not enough to trust simply to the Catholic sense of a people, even fortified by grace. For popular or folk culture tends to become distorted and to run to extremes. But what distinguishes, or ought to distinguish, a popular culture from a purely folk culture is its relationship with the high culture of its civilization. Except in the unfortunate instances in which a nation has been conquered and subjugated by another nation or warrior class different in language or manners, there will generally be a close connection between the high culture and the popular culture of a civilization. In fact, strictly speaking, they are simply two sides of the same culture, and, in general, the more closely they are related the better, as I mentioned above. This is because the popular culture needs the correcting hand of the learned to tone down its excesses and correct its errors, and the high culture needs constant contact with popular culture to prevent its becoming only a smug clique, whose standards are artificial if not perverse. Who can doubt that a healthy dose of contact with ordinary people would do much to bring sense to modern painters, sculptors, or composers? For they have forgotten the fundamental truth, that however much the arts must have an intellectual content, at the same time they must please the senses.[6] Ordinary people have never forgotten that, and rightly expect music and pictures to be pleasant to the ear or eye. But for much of today's educated class, music and art are not expected to please the senses. Instead, whatever pleasure accompanies hearing or viewing them comes from participation in a coterie of self-conscious despisers of the common herd, taking pleasure in the fact that the cultural works they admire are in fact ugly, and, therefore, displeasing to the vulgar. But though the "vulgar" are here correct, unfortunately they are more or less satisfied with the plastic products of mass culture. And the criticisms of mass culture made by those who create the esoteric modern music and art are largely correct, for mass culture tends to debase its votaries because, instead of allowing them to participate in cultural creation and activity, it makes them passive receivers and spectators of someone else's concoctions. Moreover, the cultural products of mass culture are in themselves much inferior to those of popular or folk culture.

The healthy basis of a civilization, then, will be a high culture and a popular culture in fruitful intercourse with one another. But unless the resulting culture is permeated by the Faith it will not be Catholic, no matter how good it is on a natural basis. In order for cultural objects in the narrow sense, that is, works of literature, art, and music, to be Catholic, there is one indispensable condition: This is that the life of the people, or culture in the broad sense, be Catholic. For unless the thoughts, ideals, strivings, and hopes of a nation are circumscribed and informed by Catholic faith, their cultural objects (narrow sense) cannot be Catholic. If there are no supernatural motives and no public acknowledgment of supernatural motives among a people, except perhaps a tiny minority, then the literature and art of that people will perforce portray people acting from other than supernatural motives. If all their motives, or all those they will publicly acknowledge, are on a naturalistic level, such as desire for happiness, love, sex, security, money, power, and fame; and desire for God, love of the common good, and fear of Hell are implicitly considered quaint if not insane, then their literature will be full of characters moved by the same cravings, and their art and songs will witness only to the naturalistic or secular. It is true that in a society becoming Christianized the arts can do much to form a Catholic consciousness among the people, but that is only because there already is a vital if nascent Catholic culture present. But art and literature require a social context, and it is unlikely that much genuine Catholic literature will be produced without some kind of Catholic culture or subculture. Of course, in a secular culture it is possible for Catholic writers to use naturalistic motives in their characters to demonstrate the insufficiency and falsity of life without God, as so many from Mauriac to Flannery O'Connor have done.[7] But that is not Catholic literature for a Catholic people. It may be the easiest way for 20th-century Western man to be led toward the Faith, but it is not what should be normal within the household of Faith. It is far from Medieval or other Catholic literature, in which the entire scope of Catholic truth is assumed and that wonderful mingling of the divine and the human, so characteristic of Catholic culture, is ever present.

Just as in the economic and technological spheres there is need for certain natural conditions without which the best Catholic efforts to maintain a culture cannot succeed, so also in the matter of culture in the narrow sense. Mass culture must be eliminated and high culture brought into a fruitful relationship with popular culture. This is the essential precondition for the flourishing of Catholic art and literature. When this natural good has been secured, then Catholic culture must be able to arise, reflecting the Catholic sensibilities of a Catholic people, and made fast by the stable girding of a high culture and a popular culture aiding one another. And that which is of grace must be built on that which is of nature, for the structure is not complete without both. Thus the task of decentralizing culture can go hand in hand with that of evangelizing. These are, in fact, two of the most urgent and important tasks for our time. But only the Catholic can understand the connection between them, the end which both together will support, namely, the establishment of a true Catholic civilization.

NOTES

[1] There can also be totalitarian mass culture, whose ends are political and social rather than monetary, but which uses the same means of propagation to reach the greatest number of people.

[2] There is an interesting passage in Plato's *Republic* beginning at 476b that I think is relevant here. I give the passage from Allan Bloom's translation (New York: Basic Books, 1968) pp. 156-157.

"The lover of hearing and the lovers of sights, on the one hand," I said, *"surely delight in fair sounds and colors and shapes and all that craft makes from such things, but their thought is unable to see and delight in the nature of the fair itself."*

"That," he said, *"is certainly so."*

"Wouldn't, on the other hand, those who are able to approach the fair itself and see it by itself be rare?"

"Indeed they would."

"Is the man who holds that there are fair things but doesn't hold that there is beauty itself and who, if someone leads him to the knowledge of it, isn't able to follow — is he, in your opinion, living in a dream or is he awake? Consider it. Doesn't dreaming, whether one is asleep or awake, consist in believing a likeness of something to be not a likeness, but rather the thing itself to which it is like?"

"I, at least," he said, *"would say that a man who does that dreams."*

"And what about the man who, contrary to this, believes that there is something fair itself and is able to catch sight both of it and of what participates in it, and doesn't believe that what participates is it itself, nor that it itself is what participates — is he, in your opinion, living in a dream or is he awake?"

"He's quite awake," he said.

"Wouldn't we be right in saying that this man's thought, because he knows, is knowledge, while the other's is opinion because he opines?"

The interesting thing about this discussion is that in Plato's city those who can see the fair itself and thus have knowledge, and those who see only different fair objects and thus have only opinion, are nevertheless united in admiring the same thing, but in a different manner and degree. The common citizenry of the city, who have only opinion, and the city's rulers, who have knowledge, are united because they both have the same object of delight, according to their capacity. This is very like what I think is the proper connection between high and popular culture; the same ideals but in different measure.

[3] Encyclical *Rerum Novarum*, no. 35. Translation from *Seven Great Encyclicals* (New York: Paulist, 1963) pp. 22-23.

[4] Encyclical *Quadragesimo Anno*, no. 79. Translation from *Seven Great Encyclicals*, p. 147.

[5] I am speaking here of the controllers of mass culture, executives of record companies and the like. Of the attitudes of the creators and performers of mass culture, I have no opinion.

[6] Austin J. App's *The True Concept of Literature* (San Antonio:

Mission Press, 1948) formulates very clearly the way in which literature, and by extension, all the arts, contain and convey this intellectual
content. See especially pp. 1-11. This book is little-known but contains much fine material.

7 Or the Catholic writer in a non-Catholic culture can write historical
fiction, setting his characters in a Catholic past. Thus Sigrid Undset in
her two epics was able to create Catholic characters and settings for
20th-century secular Scandinavia.

4.
For Us Men
and for Our Salvation

The need is now imperative for a renewed sense of incarnate Catholicism, of the Faith as atmosphere, as ethos, as social manifestation, as sacramental reality.

— Karl Schmude[1]

Every subject, every art or craft, has its own legitimate principles of conduct or development. Shoemaking, for example, has its own intrinsic rules proper to itself, by which it is fully able to fulfill its particular function. It would be improper for another art or science, even theology or philosophy, to dictate to the craft of shoemaking something within the purview of the latter, e.g., how to punch out leather. No other subject, no matter how excellent, has a right to say anything to shoemaking about the making of shoes as such. In this sense shoemaking is fully autonomous. But in other ways it is far from being autonomous, for the art of shoemaking is concerned with only one thing, how to make shoes. And since shoes do not exist for their own sake, but for the sake of our feet, it is only the medical art which fully understands why shoes are made and which gives to shoemaking the principles which must govern its activity, e.g., the foot's need for protection, arch support, etc. Shoemaking as such knows only vaguely, if at all, why shoes are made, since it does not understand the foot's structure or medical needs. It receives from the medical art and science the medical knowledge that it needs to guide its own proper activity, but it does not fully comprehend that knowledge.

The knowledge that shoemaking possesses, then, is part of a hierarchical series, in which one art or body of knowledge serves another, all of which in turn serve man. And in other respects also shoemaking is part of a hierarchy. In all matters concerning the common good of society it is subject to the community's provision for such matters. The place of shoemaking in the economy of the nation, the effect of the price of shoes on the common good — these are matters on which shoemaking as such knows nothing. Similarly, if the political authorities forbid a shoemaker to keep his shop open on Sundays, that is within their competence, and the shoemaker *qua* shoemaker can say nothing about this either way. This is a matter for those charged with the common good of the society. All the different elements, facets, and sectors of a community are interrelated and gathered together in a hierarchy of rights, duties, and commands, all to serve the common good of the nation as a whole, which ultimately, is the salvation of each member of society, but more immediately and directly is the establishment of conditions which both allow and encourage people to lead lives both fully human and fully Christian. If this condition is to obtain in a nation, then everything in its life must be subordinated to this goal. This by no means indicates a totalitarian aim, as I hope to make clear, but a nation in which everyone realizes that no department of life is outside of Christ.

There are, then, two ways in which each art, science, or function should be performed in such a society. First, it must seek its own specific technical excellence: the shoemaker must make good shoes for his customers, the shoes best suited to their needs. But secondly, he must do this, and must conduct the other aspects of his work, in such a way that he contributes to, or at least does not detract from, the overall purposes of the society. Four areas of life in society will be dealt with in this chapter: the political, the economic, the natural, and the sacral. These four heads include enough different examples to sketch more fully the kind of society and mode of living that best characterizes a Catholic culture.

a. Political

Politics must be included in any discussion of the common good of a society. By politics I mean the activity of those authorities who are responsible for shaping the entire common good of the people, namely, the government, the state, "the supreme arbiter, ruling in queenly fashion far above all party contention, intent only upon justice and the common good."[2] This quotation from *Quadragesimo Anno* is important because of the tendency of Americans to think of the state as a necessary evil, as merely a drain upon the productive resources of the nation, contributing nothing and taking everything. Similarly, many think of politics as simply the sordid business of power grabbing, log-rolling, and deceit, that too often seems to be the main activity of those holding governmental power, or aspiring to it. But such conceptions of the state and of politics are not distinctly formed, and the judgments resulting from them are wrong.

Politics is essentially the ordering of things in a state toward the common good. Everything has a purpose; for example, military science aims at victory in battle; rhetoric at persuasion, etc. But the ends of most of these arts are not sought for their own sake, but for other reasons, and these in turn for still others. But in that case, as Aristotle argues,

If, then, there is some end of the things we do, which we
desire for its own sake (everything else being desired for the
sake of this), and if we do not choose everything for the sake
of something else (for at that rate the process would go on to
infinity, so that our desire would be empty and vain), clearly
this must be the good and the chief good.[3]

This, Aristotle argues, is politics. This is not to say that the daily
business of running a state, or still less, of office seeking, is to
be sought for its own sake. Rather, the ends of all the other arts
are to be found in the ends of politics, which is the common
good of all.

And politics . . . is this that ordains which of the sciences
should be studied in a state, and which each class of citizens
should learn and up to what point they should learn them; and
we see even the most highly esteemed of capacities to fall
under this, e.g. strategy, economics, rhetoric; now, since
politics uses the rest of the sciences, and since, again, it
legislates as to what we are to do and what we are to abstain
from, the end of this science must include those of the others,
so that this end must be the good for man.[4]

The directing of the natural end of man, inasmuch as he lives in
society, is the subject of politics, or, to put it another way, the
deliberation about the common good, with associated means
and subordinate ends. Aristotle is simply pointing out that
matters such as the economy, the armed forces, education, etc.,
are subject to the laws, because the laws are supposed to be
framed with the good of the whole in mind, balancing and taking
into account all the particular means and ends that make up the
common good, whereas all the other arts and activities Aristotle
mentions, such as strategy, economics, rhetoric, are concerned
only with a subordinate or partial good. A government can make
laws on economic matters, but business firms do not properly
dictate to the nation's rulers. The guardianship of the common

good which rulers must exercise thus necessarily extends to all that is done in the community, but it does not follow from this that the state is omnicompetent, or superior to the Church, or that it may make laws contrary to God's law or infringe on the due liberty of its citizens.

Politics in the classical meaning, then, is the shaping of the society with reference to the common good.[5] Important matters such as education are thus very much political matters, since they are intimately involved with the society's good, and it is foolish to urge, as is sometimes done, that they should be considered "nonpolitical."

The tasks of those who hold the guardianship of the common good in a state are numerous but specific; they cannot be expanded indefinitely without trespassing onto the sphere of some other element in the culture, such as the family or the Church. From these numerous concerns of the state, however, I have chosen three to discuss in detail: laws regulating closing for religious holidays, prohibition of trading with the enemy, and censorship. Each of these examples illustrates well, I think, the function of the state as chief guardian of the common good of a culture.

The first two of these functions involve regulation of the economy. In a genuinely Catholic society the various elements in the economy would be formed into self-governing vocational groups, reminiscent of the medieval guilds, and subject to only general supervision by the state. Many matters that are now handled by departments of the government, such as working conditions, hours of work, conditions of apprenticeship, etc., would be matters for the particular vocational group concerned instead. Thus the government would have little direct control of economic affairs, but the organized vocational groups would be, as it were, the community's agents for seeing that all sectors of the economy conducted their business so as to serve the community and contribute to the common good.[6] Yet some matters transcend one industry or field of work. Both closing for religious holidays and prohibiting trading with foreign enemies are among these. Though the second of these is nearly universally accepted, and the first was widely so until recently, both prohibitions exemplify clearly the supremacy of the interests of society as a whole over the private profit of individuals and over their economic freedom. That is, to accept either of them is logically to accept the proposition that whenever the common good of the community will be harmed by an individual's economic activity, then that economic activity may be licitly restricted or prohibited. Both the practice of normal buying and selling on Sundays and other holy days of obligation,[7] and traitorous commerce with an enemy of the state are contrary to the common good, because both, in different measure, will destroy the state and what it stands for, i.e., the life of a people in a Catholic culture. The logic of the primacy of considerations about the common good of the culture can be built up quite easily from a foundation of these two prohibitions, so that, if anything can be shown to have a deleterious effect on the society, there must be a means, direct or indirect, to regulate or prohibit it. To conceive that the political order must stand helpless in the face of threats to the well-being of the nation, because the economic order is considered inviolable, is to make an erroneous judgment on the place and purpose of economic activity. Any rulers who have watched their nation deteriorate because of injustice or turmoil caused by economic activity and done nothing have abdicated their responsibility. If the parents of a family refused to stop certain actions of their children that were tearing the family apart because of mistaken beliefs about the limits of parental authority, we would call them foolish or cowardly. It is the same in a state. Though there are real limits to state authority, as to parental, the Lockean state of the 19th and early 20th centuries did not fulfill its obligations, but allowed economic life to go its own way in violation of the common good.[8] Today, when the state is more cognizant of its proper role in economic affairs (though its manner of acting frequently violates the principle of subsidiarity) it has abdicated to an even greater extent its necessary task of cultural[9] supervision, that is, censorship.

Just as economic restraint by the state in the interests of the common good enrages those who call themselves conservatives, so cultural restraint, or censorship, enrages liberals. Since I am dealing here with Catholic culture I will discuss the type of censorship proper to a Catholic society, which will include, but go beyond, the kind which ought to be engaged in by liberal democracies. Thus a Catholic state will properly censor not only pornography, but everything tending to undermine the society, including works advocating opinions and theories which contradict society's order of beliefs.

Censorship illustrates well the dependence of the individual on society and his lack of a right to undermine any society insofar as it is founded on truth. The individual is neither autonomous nor supreme, and he has no right to absolute freedom either in moneymaking or in cultural pursuits. Society has a right to order both areas toward the common good.

Censorship currently has a very bad name in the West, and this, I think, chiefly for two reasons. First, most people whose opinions are noticed and influence others no longer believe that we really know any truths, or even that there is a possibility of knowing any truths, especially truths in the moral order — an idea immediately traceable to the philosopher Immanuel Kant. Any rational defense of censorship, on the other hand, must make the argument that since the state takes steps to protect the community from menaces to its physical health, similarly it should take steps to protect the community from menaces to its intellectual or spiritual health. For manifestly, ideas lead to action, and bad ideas will thus lead to bad acts, bringing hurt to individuals and potential ruin to the community. But this presupposes that we really know what is good and what is bad, something that many of our contemporaries profess to doubt.[10] And it follows from this doubt, that if we do censor we are as likely to be suppressing a newfound truth as restraining a destructive error.

The second reason why censorship is so ill regarded is because of what in logic is called the fallacy of the particular instance. Some notable examples of censorship in the past, particularly the Galileo case, have persuaded liberals that censors are always narrow-minded and opposed to any new ideas, whether true or false. The fact that many of those initiating censorship attempts in schools and libraries are uneducated and parochial, and have sometimes attempted to censor authors such as Chaucer and Shakespeare, further convinces the opponents of censorship that only an ignorant bigot could favor banning books. This, as I said, is a fallacious line of argument, for it does not follow that censorship in itself, or every instance of censorship, is wrong just because many censors or would-be censors have acted stupidly or unjustly. The uneducated and parochial, moreover, have taken upon themselves this very necessary task of censorship by default, since those of more learning and experience are unwilling to do the job. The unlearned see that it needs to be done, so they take it upon themselves to do it, very poorly it is true, but they cannot be entirely blamed, since they have been largely abandoned by those who have the necessary knowledge and experience and should know how to do it better. But since censorship would be a respected task in a Catholic state, it would not be left to the ignorant and inexperienced, nor would it (any more than any other human activity) be carried out inexpertly or stupidly. Obviously in universities a liberal education must be given, and cannot be given without the reading of many books containing much erroneous teaching. But that is a risk one has to take, and such safeguards as are proper and possible will considerably diminish the danger. Moreover, one must not confuse the norms of Catholic literature with those of

Victorian prudes.[11] Medieval literature contained many scatological and sexual references, and the prohibition of pornography need not mean that literature is made to conform to the conventions of the Bible belt.

Censorship, then, illustrates the necessity for the individual to be restrained, in the interests of the common good, in his cultural expression. Just as in economic matters the stability of society is not compatible with profit-seeking free of the constraints which should channel economic activity toward the common good, so intellectual or aesthetic activity cannot be allowed to subvert the truths that a culture embodies. Those who fear that censorship will dry up the springs of cultural life forget that almost all literature and art up to, and in some cases beyond, the 19th century, was produced under some form of state or ecclesiastical censorship, yet great literary and artistic activity was obviously not lacking. If man and his life are to be the primary consideration in what is the good for society, then he and his way of life must be protected from false beliefs which, along with the strife produced by economic greed, is the surest way to erode a culture's foundations.

b. Economic

In the first chapter I discussed at some length the connection between economic activity, particularly the point of view with which it is carried on, and the life of man in society. Here I will only briefly mention a few of the concrete ways a society would order its economic activity to insure that it was in harmony with both the immediate and ultimate ends of society.

In the first place, the key toward insuring that economic activity respects the common good is the establishment of a vocational order in commerce and industry. This is an arrangement in which those working in the same profession or industry, regardless of position on the labor market or level of work, are united on the basis of their common task of fulfilling a function needed by society, either producing a product or performing a service. The entire orientation of their work must be toward the fulfillment of their function as a service to society. Of course they will make their living by their service, and in some cases may even grow rich, but the public external structure of their activity (as distinguished from their secret thoughts, over which society has no control) must always be directed toward supplying a need of society. That is, the vocational group as a whole, and the individual firms or owners that comprise it, would not make maximization of profits their purpose, either directly or indirectly, but rather service to the community. The vocational group by its regulations would institutionalize this orientation toward the common good, and moreover, would tend to mitigate competition, since all the groups involved in the industry in question, labor, management, owners, all individual firms, would share in decision-making about common matters. These groups, which would have a public legal status and not be merely voluntary organizations, would deliberate on matters such as wages, prices, working conditions, etc. Not all such decisions would necessarily be binding on those involved in a particular industry or profession; the freedom of the individual firm would be preserved to the extent necessary and desirable. Beyond this, little that is definite can be said, for the popes do not specify the exact role or structure of vocational orders, leaving much to circumstances of time and place.[12] The main point to be grasped is that the political authority would invest the self-governing vocational group with public legal authority in order to orient the economy toward the common good without excessive direct state intervention. The individual could expect the opportunity to make his living by his work, but he could not expect the opportunity to grow rich,[13] especially if the means of doing so involved harmful speculation or any other practice contrary to economic stability. Some of course would grow rich anyway, and if they did so without upsetting the stability of the culture, then no one could object.[14] But the principal considerations for those making decisions on economic matters should always be: How will this affect the common good, what will this do to the economic structure of society, what will happen in the everyday life of ordinary people? If questions such as these are kept in mind, then economic activity will fulfill its important task of providing the necessary goods and services to people without subjecting them to the stress and dislocation of an economy in continual turmoil.

Moreover, a Catholic society would order its laws to promote widespread property ownership by rich and poor alike. This ownership would preferably be as single proprietors, but in the case of large concerns would necessarily take the form of ownership by the workers involved. All these points have been the subject of numerous papal urgings.[15]

c. Natural

It is among the cardinal principles of Catholic theology that grace completes nature; it does not destroy it. Thus things and processes have natural perfections, that is, a completeness or correctness according to their own natures, apart from (though not in opposition to) divine grace. I mentioned this above with reference to shoemaking. The perfection of things that more intimately concern man, such as customs and practices concerning birth and death, love and marriage, housing, etc., is ordered to the perfection, both natural and supernatural, of man, for these things are meant to serve man. Now the human good of man should be secured as well as the divine. Of course, if one has to choose, it is better to get a man to Heaven than to feed him on earth, but it is better by far to do both, and both are subjects of our Lord's commands.

Some might think that the practices surrounding giving birth, for example, are thoroughly human and thoroughly Catholic if the birth is as safe as the medical art can make it, the mother receives all the normal blessings of the Church before and after birth, and the baby is baptized within a few weeks after the birth. These, of course, are all necessary and laudable, but there is another facet not included: What is the total effect of the birth on the mother and father as individuals, as a couple, on the family as a whole, on society? About twenty-five or thirty years ago many women and their husbands began to think that the birth practices then prevailing in America — treating every normal birth as a high-risk delivery, routinely subjecting both mother and baby to many practices which were not only unnecessary, costly, and sometimes dangerous, but had absolutely no respect for the family as a whole — were both unnecessary and harmful. As is well known, the situation has greatly changed in most places since then. Now, hospital birthing rooms, home births, prepared "natural" deliveries, and many such practices are common. Is all this simply a fad with no significance for the Catholic? I do not think so, for the new or newly revived birth practices are very much more consonant with the human perfection of man, and thus more in harmony with the supernatural also, than the "traditional" methods. God did not intend that a mother, in a routine low-risk delivery, be drugged, separated from her spouse, unable to see the joyous moment when her newborn emerges into the world.[16] Nor did He intend that the husband be separated from his wife, unable to provide support to her or welcome to his child. The revolt by couples against this hospital regimentation was mainly a natural revolt, that is, one based on a correct perception of human nature and its needs, not especially associated with divine grace or the Church.[17] But since it is true to human nature, it is good. For even in a Catholic society, in which most people are normally in a state of grace and have many supernatural motives for living good lives, it is wrong and it is stupid to expect people to accept arrangements that disregard and outrage their humanity. It is wrong because it does harm to people, places obstacles in their paths, and overturns God's order of things; it is stupid because grace completes nature, it does not replace it, and most of us will resist temptation more easily if our supernatural motives are supported by natural foundations, or at least not hindered by them. For example, if it is true that the getting acquainted or "bonding" of a mother and her newborn in the minutes and hours immediately after birth produces good effects throughout life in the relations of the mother and child, why deprive the family of this added help by carting the baby off to the nursery or drugging one or both of them? True, bonding is not as important as the supernatural charity that should bind parents and children together, but why should the natural be disregarded, since it was God who created it, and reliance placed solely on the supernatural? It is not the Catholic way to ignore the natural patterns and order that God has created. Whatever is really human should thereby be of interest to the Catholic, and must be incorporated into a Catholic culture.

It is not only in practices surrounding giving birth that the specifically human must be sought, but in many other cases as well. Is the custom of the siesta, for example, merely an adaptation to living in hot climates, or is it also an ingenious way of encouraging fathers to return home for lunch and participate for a few hours in the family? a way of slowing down the hasty rush of business life? This custom, and the office and work hours based on it, fosters a different attitude toward both work and leisure, an attitude that I think is probably more in accord with Catholicism than the one we have. This is a matter deserving further thought.[18]

Do our individualistic dating customs encourage a prudent choice of a mate, or do they make it more likely that merely superficial qualities will be considered, parental advice ignored, and the idea promoted that love is essentially a feeling, and one not subject to the moral law either? Do our practices of house building, and the economic arrangements behind them, encourage or discourage large families? Extended families? Does our highway building and our town planning encourage or discourage stable neighborhoods and parishes, places where families can be raised, where real organic social life is possible?[19] Do our North American funeral customs direct people's minds toward the four last things, or do they attempt to disguise death in a mass of semi-pagan trappings?[20] All these things — though they might seem to some basically indifferent — are important if a culture is to be permeated with a Catholic spirit. As Fr. Bull wrote, "the whole realm of unspoken and spontaneous things, which color even our daily routine" must be made Catholic, must point us toward Christ, must help us gain Heaven.

There are many other customs and practices that can be made either better or worse, either more Catholic or less so. The point is that the standard we use to judge such customs and practices must not be that of material productivity or cost. We must realize that such practices are meant to serve the same ends as economic activity and technology, namely, the right living of individuals, families, and communities in society, which in turn is to serve the eternal salvation of these same individuals. Only if we subsume everything under this goal can we begin to judge correctly, for otherwise we scarcely know what anything is for. All things must be restored in Christ, and neither the least nor the smallest of our pursuits or arrangements can be excepted.

d. Sacral

The final element of life that I take up in this chapter is what I call the sacral, or more properly, the sacralizing of all of life, the intermingling, mostly spontaneous and unplanned, of the sacred with the secular. There are certain obvious ways in which this can be done, some of which were mentioned in the Introduction. The placing of holy water fonts at doors of shops and houses, not simply of churches; the placing of shrines and religious statues along roads and in squares and parks; the giving of religious names, such as saints' names, to streets, houses, bridges, and the like; and the holding of public religious festivals and processions, are some of the ways. By such means religion, that the fact that there is a God, that He became incarnate and died for us and rose again, and all the truths of the Faith can be brought out from the church building and placed among us as we go about our daily tasks. Regardless of the kind of culture in which we dwell, we can make Christ present in our daily lives by turning our minds to Him in short prayers and aspirations. But He wishes to be present not only in our inner selves and minds, but outwardly among us in the world. And if our public life, our life outside our churches and homes, is devoid of any reminders of Him, we make His presence among us more difficult to discern.

One very important part of the sacralizing of public life involves the liturgy and the Church year. The liturgy must be seen as central, that ·which above all binds a Catholic culture together. The sacrifice of the Mass is the bond among Catholics, and must never be considered as peripheral to real life.[21] Thus the parish organization is not just a convenient administrative district of the Church, but part of Christ's Mystical Body, that cell, as it were, in which Catholics are grouped around the unity of the sacramental life. The village or country district, the section of a larger town or city, must find its unity in the parish church, around the Eucharistic Lord.

If this is the place of the liturgy, it follows that the Church year must have a governing role in cultural and social life. Advent, for example, cannot be merely something which occurs within the church building, something merely ecclesiastical, while outside and in our homes we have already begun the celebration of Christmas.[22] Nor can Easter, for a Catholic, begin two weeks before Good Friday with the placing of an idol of the Easter bunny in some store or shopping mall. The practice of observing the liturgical year only in the church building, while outside following the secular holiday customs, involves an unbelievable bifurcation of the Catholic mind, a frank acceptance of the proposition that religion has really nothing to do with ordinary life, and a subordination of our Catholicism to whatever our culture happens to propose for our observance. Clearly if all cultural activity is subordinate to the Faith, the rhythm of the Church's year must be the guide for our festivities. Holiday is only a changed spelling for holy day, and in a Catholic culture the two must be made one again. The festivals of the saints must again become our days of rest and rejoicing, and if we desire to institute special times of mourning or remembrance for those killed in war, or for giving thanks, or for any other reason, why can this not be incorporated within the existing structure of the Church year? For example, All Souls, or the feast of some soldier-saint, are obvious days to remember war dead; the feast of St. Martin of Tours (November 11) was the original day in Europe for giving thanks for a good harvest, a custom that was Protestantized in the Pilgrim's Thanksgiving Day,[23] the ancestor of our present state religious holiday of Thanksgiving, the only "holy day" instituted by the government. In a Catholic culture it will be natural to connect our profound desires to honor our dead or celebrate some event with our Faith; indeed, it is unnatural for a Catholic ever to separate them. Thus it will be natural to make use, as much as possible, of existing Church festivals for commemorations, instead of instituting some new merely political or civic holiday, an excessive number of which obscure the fact that the Church year ought to be observed in the square as well as in the sanctuary. If we have more feeling for our dead on Memorial Day than on All Souls, does not this indicate how far we have absorbed secular American modes of thought and feeling, and abandoned Catholic thinking? If so, then, this is just another indication of our need of a Catholic culture if we are to fully live and think as Catholics.

The observance of the Christian year and the open display of religious symbols, then, serve to remind us that Christ is real, that He is King, and that He is, or ought to be, a part of our daily lives and our daily work. The lack of a crucifix on the wall of a shop does not insure that its owner will overcharge his customers or sell shoddy goods, but it is worth remarking that in fact the denuding of northern Europe of public religious symbols coincided with the rise of the economic theory that elevated private greed into a law of nature. The sacralization of society does more, however, than remind us that we too will die; it helps make clear society's corporate commitment to Christ and the Catholic faith, and it tends to prevent that fatal compartmentalized intellect that is so common in the modern world, and so forms in us a Catholic mind.

Each of us has in his mind certain ruling ideas[24] which, though largely subconscious, tend to make us react in definite ways to propositions, ideas, proposals, and even words and terms we encounter. Because of these ruling ideas of ours we respond in a reflex manner. For example, we are apt to have such subconscious reflex judgments as: leisure is justified only if it is a storing up of energy for more work; or, old ideas are generally less valuable than new ideas; or, material progress is necessarily good; or, the poor are morally inferior to the rich; or, activity is its own justification. Unless we have been extremely careful and taken measures to guard ourselves, we most probably have picked up some or all of the above from our surrounding non-Catholic culture. And when any idea is presented to us we respond to it on two levels, one with our fully conscious minds, the other on the subconscious level, and the latter tends to color the former's acts.

Our subconscious acceptance of such reflex judgments can manifest itself in unexpected ways. A subconscious bias in favor of material progress might take the form of favoring one kind of educational curriculum over another, because the first was oriented toward more immediate practical uses, while the other seemed unduly preoccupied with speculative knowledge, or in favoring solutions to the problems of poor countries that assume their development must follow the pattern of North America and Europe. This same bias can predispose one to regard modern civilization as manifestly superior to any earlier civilization. A high school chemistry textbook of mine stated this explicitly when it said that, because of its utility in industrial processes, the level of civilization in a nation could be gauged by the amount of sulfuric acid it consumed! I suspect that many moderns would pass by this identification of civilization with industrialization with no recognition of its underlying philosophic materialism.

But even mere terms and words can affect our thinking. When we hear such terms as "social justice," "the poor," "the common good," "work," "leisure," hardly adverting to their meaning and significance, we react to them and our thinking takes off in a certain direction because of this reaction. We can test this on ourselves by playing the parlor game of free association, seeing what word pops into our heads when these and other key terms from Catholic thought are mentioned. I believe that most of us will find that Protestant and secularist assumptions have influenced us more than we had realized.

What is the remedy for this? It is twofold. First, to form the habit of always reasoning back to first principles, for this will enable one to avoid the worst consequences of any non-Catholic coloration of one's thinking, if one rigorously presses the argument back to its beginnings. But in the long run it is also necessary to acquire a Catholic mind, both conscious and subconscious, for we do not always have the time or mental strength to push our reasoning back to its ultimate premises. One formed in a Catholic culture will acquire a Catholic mind the same way we pick up non-Catholic mental reflexes, effortlessly and unwittingly. We who live in non-Catholic cultures must attempt to reason always from first principles, and at the same time to try to form the Catholic mind in ourselves, chiefly by wide reading in Catholic books, especially those which are the products of genuine Catholic cultures or in touch with a living Catholic tradition, for not every book which is dogmatically unobjectionable is wholly free from the subconscious prejudices of Protestantized secularism. The end that we seek is a mind whose bounds and landmarks are the doctrines of Christ — that the last shall be first, that the poor are blessed, that we must seek first His kingdom and His justice — a mind that habitually rejects whatever is foreign to Christ's mind and alien to His teachings.

Another phenomenon, connected with this, is the curious fact that many men, even Catholics, are ashamed to admit, or loath to accept, motives that are not materialist. For example, one might accept that a certain thing should not be done because it would cost too much or might get one into trouble with the civil authorities. But the fact that it is against the moral law or is dishonorable — these one is ashamed to speak of. If we find that a proposed course of action which is immoral is also financially disadvantageous — how happy we are, for we now have a reason against it we are not ashamed to bring up. For we are ill at ease in arguing a case on any other ground than the financial or legal, and whatever vague notions we have of the better reasons we do not even know how to properly formulate. A realistic attitude is equated with a hard-boiled one, and it is forgotten that realism consists in accepting and acting on what is and what is most important — surely the fact that one will live forever in Heaven or Hell, not that one might lose such and such amount of money or even go to prison. But of course, too much of this kind of realism is not considered productive, and can usually be sneered into silence.

The world is constantly pushing in on us, and though a Catholic culture is no substitute for prayer, the sacraments, and personal sanctity, it is a help for these and a good in itself, and one that we cannot afford to despise. Of course, many of the practices I have included under the categories of natural and sacral cannot be established by the state nor by any other organized body. Much will have to result from a slow diffusion of organic Catholicity among a people, aided where possible and prudent by the gentle action of organized bodies. But where a people is truly Catholic, and is not hindered by anything external, this slow diffusion will occur. As Karl Schmude wrote in his very interesting article, "In Praise of the Catholic People,"

> Wherever Catholicism has struck root in a society, it has cultivated a living and sympathetic sense of the ordinary life. In each case it has given rise to a particular social climate and ethos, a distinctive style of life: in each case it has given rise to a Catholic people.[25]

A Catholic people — a Catholic culture — this is what we must try to form, not as our ultimate purpose, for that is always Heaven, but as a nearly indispensible means for attaining the kind of life we were meant to live on earth, and an aid and support for the journey to the lasting city that we are seeking, both for ourselves and for all our kindred in Christ.

NOTES

[1] "In Praise of the Catholic People," *Homiletic & Pastoral Review*, November 1978, p. 15.

[2] Encyclical *Quadragesimo Anno*, no. 109. Translation from *Seven Great Encyclicals* (New York: Paulist, 1963) p. 154.

[3] Aristotle, *Nicomachean Ethics*, I, 2. (Oxford translation)

[4] *Ibid.*

[5] The ordinary sense of "politics," as meaning the activity of politicians and political parties, is really not a different thing altogether, and is related to the classical sense as a kind of deviation from the norm. That is, politicians exist only because they are thought to make some contribution to the common good. And in spite of corruption and stupidity, they do more good than harm, otherwise we would be better off without any government at all than with our present one, something obviously not the case. The formal and public orientation of the politicians' activity, then, is toward the common good, which is why politicians in their public statements justify their actions as contributions to the common good. This shows that both we and they regard that as their real reason for existing, despite our justified cynicism and their unjustified self-seeking and corruption. The proper way, then, to regard politics in the ordinary meaning is as something partially perverted from its essential end, rather than as something different and having no connection with the classical meaning.

[6] Cf. the discussion in chapter 1.

[7] Although Sundays and other holy days of obligation are set apart from ordinary occupations, neither canon law nor Catholic tradition has regarded Sunday in the narrow way that the Puritan tradition does. Work has been prohibited, not recreation or play.

[8] Encyclical *Rerum Novarum*, nos. 2, 26-29. Encyclical *Quadragesimo Anno*, nos. 4, 25-28, 109-110.

[9] I use culture in its narrow sense throughout this discussion of censorship. Cf. chapter 3.

[10] Yet at the same time secularists seem to have no difficulty in asserting that some things definitely are wrong. They perceive the evil of racism, for example, and do not allow the possibility that it might not be an evil. But this seems hard to reconcile with their fundamental epistemological skepticism.

[11] For an excellent discussion of this matter, see Austin J. App, *The True Concept of Literature* (San Antonio: Mission Press, 1948) pp. 17-56.

[12] Cf. Encyclical *Quadragesimo Anno*, nos. 65, 82-90. The litera-ture on the subject of vocational groups is voluminous, much of it not in English. But see especially, Richard Arès, *What is Corporative Organization* (St. Louis: Central Bureau, 1939); Charles P. Bruehl, *The Pope's Plan for Social Reconstruction* (New York: Devin-Adair, 1939); Mary Lois Eberdt & Gerald J. Schnepp, *Industrialism and the Popes* (New York: P. J. Kenedy, 1953); Oswald von Nell-Breuning, *Reorganization of Social Economy* (Milwaukee: Bruce, 1936).

[13] Cf. John A. Ryan, *Distributive Justice*, 3rd ed. (New York: Macmillan, 1942) p. 223.

[14] Some of the Medieval guilds, however, actually set a limit on the amount of wealth their members could possess. Ryan argues that a legal limitation on wealth is licit but imprudent. cf. *Distributive Justice*, 3rd ed., pp. 224-227.

[15] Encyclical *Rerum Novarum*, nos. 4, 10, 26, 35; Encyclical *Quad-ragesimo Anno*, nos. 59-62, 65; Encyclical *Mater et Magistra*, nos. 85-89, 91-93, 111-115; Encyclical *Laborem Exercens*, no. 14. See also the excellent book by Hilaire Belloc, *The Restoration of Property* (New York: Sheed & Ward, 1946).

[16] Cf. John 16:21.

[17] Catholic moral theologians, however, did warn against the in-discriminate use of drugs in normal childbirth; cf. Edwin F. Healy, *Moral Guidance*, 2nd ed. (Chicago: Loyola University, 1960) p. 272.

In addition, Catholic manuals for married couples regularly recom-mended breastfeeding of babies during the time when it was least practiced in North America; cf. Philip Christopher M. Kelly, *The Catholic Book of Marriage* (New York: Farrar, Straus & Young, 1951) p. 105; Henry V. Sattler, *Parents, Children and the Facts of Life* (Paterson, NJ: St. Anthony's Guild, 1953) pp. 125-126; Edwin F. Healy, *Medical Ethics* (Chicago: Loyola University, 1956) p. 324; George A. Kelly, *The Catholic Marriage Manual* (New York: Ran-dom House, 1958) pp. 70-72. La Leche League, the worldwide organ-ization that encourages and helps mothers to nurse their infants, was founded in 1956 by Catholic mothers and named after Nuestra Senora de la Leche y Buen Parto, a shrine of Our Blessed Lady in St. Augustine, Florida. Here, as in many other instances, the best aspects of the counter-culture of the 60s and early 70s were already contained in Catholic thought; cf. my article, "Catholics and the Bourgeois Mind," *Social Justice Review* 74 (September-October 1983) 147-148.

[18] There is some evidence that a human being naturally tends to feel sleepy in the early or mid-afternoon. cf. "Napping for Energy," Uni-versity of California, Berkeley, *Wellness Letter*, v. 2, no. 1, Oct. 1985, p.3.

[19] Cf. Jane Jacobs, *The Death and Life of Great American Cities* (New York: Vintage, 1961) and Russell Kirk, "The Architecture of Servitude and Boredom" in *Reclaiming a Patrimony* (Washington: Heritage Foundation, 1982) pp. 81-91.

[20] Cf. Jessica Mitford, *The American Way of Death* (New York: Simon & Schuster, 1963).

[21] Cf. Constitution on the Sacred Liturgy, *Sacrosanctum Concilium*, no. 10.

[22] Cf. my article, "The Two Christmases," *The Wanderer* 116 (December 22, 1983).

[23] Francis X. Weiser, *Handbook of Christian Feasts and Customs*, abridged ed. (New York: Paulist, 1963) pp. 161-162. As a matter of fact, Catholics in America regarded Thanksgiving Day as part of an alien tradition and did not observe it until 1878, when Cardinal Gibbons promoted it among Catholics. cf. Francis B. Thornton, *Our American Princes* (New York: G.P. Putnam's, 1963) pp. 55-56.

[24] I use "ideas" here to mean not only concepts, but also propositions and arguments.

[25] "In Praise of the Catholic People," p. 10.

Epilogue

A true pastoral concern will be founded on a living awareness
of the Catholic people, and on a sympathetic appreciation of
the conditions which make such a people possible — the
social and institutional milieu within which religious belief is
made credible and the religious life practicable.

— Karl Schmude[1]

A Catholic's ultimate link with the Church, as far as he is
concerned, is always his faith. It is our faith, our belief that what
the Church teaches is true, that what she looses and binds
Heaven also looses and binds — it is this that sends us to Mass
week after week, that keeps us frequenting the sacraments and
attempting to keep Christ's law, and which leads us to the
confessional when we fail. It is that which makes a man on his
deathbed send for a priest, though no sacrament has touched him
for forty years. Did we not believe the Church's preaching, what
reason would we have to continue to live as Catholics? Faith is
primary and always lies at the bottom of any motives for pleas-
ing God and living the Christian life. If this is the case, it should
follow that any conditions which foster and preserve faith ought
also to be fostered and preserved. This a Catholic culture above
all does. The process that has figured so largely in modern
history, secularization, has made faith difficult for many, because it has destroyed the external supports, the "social and
institutional milieu," which is helpful for everyone and for
many almost a necessity. If we desire the salvation of all, we

must strive to realize the conditions that promote the faith of all.

The two chief benefits which a genuine Catholic culture secures — the ready acceptance and recognition of the supernatural, and the subordination of all things to their proper ends — are obviously productive of many other goods also, both natural and supernatural. When human goods are ordered to their ends they are *ipso facto* put in proper perspective and directed to the common good. No one thing is allowed to assume more importance than it really has, because each thing is strictly subordinated to its purpose.

Moreover, certain pervasive elements of existence, such as time, directly affect how we regard many other aspects of life; e.g., in the case of time, leisure and work, youth and age, technology and the use of natural resources. Our attitude toward time even affects our attitudes toward family life, friendship, the intellectual life, the worship of God. If we misperceive the value and use of time, then we will misperceive the value and use of these other things. But a Catholic culture, because it will embody a right regard for time, will ascribe to activities and occupations which depend on time a like proper valuation and place, and will at the same time form in our souls correct estimates of all these diverse things. It will shape both our minds and the external conditions of our bodies and our lives after a manner that accords correct recognition to God and to every created thing.

A Catholic culture is thus a notable help in achieving such happiness as is possible on this earth, and in attaining the perfect happiness of the next life. Nothing can better serve man than this. The establishment of a Catholic culture is the external aspect of St. Pius X's aim "to restore all things in Christ," the necessary outward complement of Christ's reign in individual hearts. The two, of course, are intimately connected, and if the reign of natural justice in social and economic affairs cannot be firmly established unless men turn toward Christ, so much the less can a true Catholic culture be restored unless persons are willing to allow Him first place in their lives. This twofold objective, then, the individual and social reign of Christ the King, should be made the explicit aspiration of every Catholic. Let us reform our lives, let us reform our thinking, and then, perhaps, God will deign to let us see a real reshaping of civilization.

NOTES

[1] "In Praise of the Catholic People," *Homiletic & Pastoral Review*, November 1978, p. 15.

Bibliography

I. Works that deal in some way with Catholic culture or touch on one of the cultural themes discussed in this book. I do not necessarily endorse everything contained in each of these works.

Jaime Balmes. *European Civilization*, 13th ed. Baltimore: John Murphy, 1873.

Hilaire Belloc. "The Faith and Industrial Capitalism" in *Essays of a Catholic Layman in England*. New York: Macmillan, 1931.

Michael L. Berger. *The Devil Wagon in God's Country: the Automobile and Social Change in Rural America, 1893-1929*. Hamden, Conn.: Shoe String, 1979.

Ralph Adams Cram. *Walled Towns*. Boston: Marshall Jones, 1920.

Christopher Dawson. "Catholicism and the Bourgeosis Mind" in *The Dynamics of World History*. New York: Sheed and Ward, 1956.

_____. "The Patriarchal Family in History" in *The Dynamics of World History*. New York: Sheed and Ward, 1956.

Amintore Fanfani. *Catholicism, Protestantism and Capitalism*. New York: Sheed and Ward, 1939.

Jane Jacobs. *The Death and Life of Great American Cities*. New York: Vintage, 1961.

C.S. Lewis. *The Abolition of Man*. New York: Macmillan, 1947.

Michael Novak. "Catholicism, Cultural" in *New Catholic Encyclopedia*, vol. 17. Washington: Publishers Guild, 1979.

_____. *The Rise of the Unmeltable Ethnics*. New York: Macmillan, 1971.

Josef Pieper. *Leisure, the Basis of Culture*. New York: New American Library, 1963.

Amos Rapoport. *House Form and Culture*. Englewood Cliffs, N.J.: Prentice-Hall, 1969.

Fanchón Royer. "Our Town." *The Catholic World* 170 (March 1950) 432-435.

Kirkpatrick Sale. *Human scale*. New York: Coward, McCann & Geoghegan, 1980.

Karl G. Schmude. "In Praise of the Catholic People." *Homiletic & Pastoral Review*, November 1978, pp. 10-19.

E.F. Schumacher. *Good Work*. New York: Harper, 1979.

John Senior. *The Death of Christian Culture*. New Rochelle, NY: Arlington House, 1978.

_____. *The Restoration of Christian Culture*. San Francisco: Ignatius, 1983.

Richard Tawney. *Religion and the Rise of Capitalism*. New York: Harcourt, Brace, 1926.

Francis X. Weiser. *Handbook of Christian Feasts and Customs*, abridged ed. New York: Paulist, 1963.

_____. *The Year of the Lord in the Christian Home*. Collegeville, MN: Liturgical, 1964.

Benjamin Winterborn. "The Cult of Efficiency." *The Catholic Digest*, September 1980, pp. 92-94.

Alfred Young. *Catholic and Protestant Countries Compared*. New York: Catholic Book Exchange, 1895.

II. Catholic works on education

George Bull. *The Function of the Catholic College*. New York: America Press, 1933.

_____. "The Function of the Catholic Graduate School." *Thought* 13 (September 1938) 364-380.

George E. Ganss. *Saint Ignatius' Idea of a Jesuit University*. Milwaukee: Marquette University, 1954.

William T. Kane. *Catholic Library Problems*. Chicago: Loyola University, 1939.

_____. *History of Education*, rev. ed. Chicago: Loyola University, 1954.

_____. *Some Principles of Education*. Chicago: Loyola University, 1938.

III. Catholic works on politics

Augustine J. Osgniach. *The Christian State*. Milwaukee: Bruce, 1943.

Heinrich Rommen. *The State in Catholic Thought*. St. Louis: Herder, 1945.